OTHER PUBLICATIONS FROM THE DRUCKER FOUNDATION

Organizational Leadership Resource

The Drucker Foundation Self-Assessment Tool

Wisdom to Action Series

Leading Beyond the Walls, *Frances Hesselbein, Marshall Goldsmith, Iain Somerville, Editors*

The Drucker Foundation Future Series

The Leader of the Future, *Frances Hesselbein, Marshall Goldsmith, Richard Beckhard, Editors*

The Organization of the Future, *Frances Hesselbein, Marshall Goldsmith, Richard Beckhard, Editors*

The Community of the Future, *Frances Hesselbein, Marshall Goldsmith, Richard Beckhard, Richard F. Schubert, Editors*

Video Training Resources

Excellence in Nonprofit Leadership Video, *featuring Peter F. Drucker, Max De Pree, Frances Hesselbein, and Michele Hunt Moderated by Richard F. Schubert*

Lessons in Leadership Video, *with Peter F. Drucker*

Journal and Related Books

Leader to Leader (journal)

Leader to Leader: Enduring Insights on Leadership from the Drucker Foundation's Award-Winning Journal, *Frances Hesselbein, Paul Cohen, Editors*

Online Resources

www.leaderbooks.org

The Collaboration Challenge

**A DRUCKER FOUNDATION
LEADERBOOK**

ABOUT THE DRUCKER FOUNDATION

The Peter F. Drucker Foundation for Nonprofit Management, founded in 1990, takes its name and inspiration from the acknowledged father of modern management. By providing educational opportunities and resources, the foundation furthers its mission "to lead social sector organizations toward excellence in performance." It pursues this mission through the presentation of conferences, video teleconferences, the annual Peter F. Drucker Award for Nonprofit Innovation, and the annual Frances Hesselbein Community Innovation Fellows program, as well as through the development of management resources, partnerships, and publications.

Since its founding, the Drucker Foundation's special role has been to serve as a broker of intellectual capital, bringing together the finest leaders, consultants, authors, and social philosophers in the world with the leaders of social sector voluntary organizations.

The Drucker Foundation believes that a healthy society requires three vital sectors: a public sector of effective governments, a private sector of effective businesses, and a social sector of effective community organizations. The mission of the social sector and its organizations is to change lives. It accomplishes this mission by addressing the needs of the spirit, mind, and body of individuals, the community, and society. This sector and its organizations also create a meaningful sphere of effective and responsible citizenship.

The Drucker Foundation aims to make its contribution to the health of society by strengthening the social sector through the provision of intellectual resources to leaders in business, government, and the social sector. In the first nine years after its inception, the Drucker Foundation, among other things:

- Presented the Drucker Innovation Award, which each year generates several hundred applications from local community enterprises; many applicants work in fields where results are difficult to achieve.
- Worked with social sector leaders through the Frances Hesselbein Community Innovation Fellows program.
- Held twenty conferences in the United States and in countries across the world.
- Developed six books: a *Self-Assessment Tool* (revised 1998) for nonprofit organizations; three books in the Drucker Foundation Future Series, *The Leader of the Future* (1996), *The Organization of the Future* (1997), and *The Community of the Future* (1998); *Leader to Leader* (1999); and *Leading Beyond the Walls* (1999).
- Developed *Leader to Leader,* a quarterly journal for leaders from all three sectors.

For more information on the Drucker Foundation, contact:

The Peter F. Drucker Foundation for Nonprofit Management
320 Park Avenue, Third Floor
New York, NY 10022-6839 U.S.A.
Telephone: (212) 224-1174
Fax: (212) 224-2508
E-mail: info@pfdf.org
Web address: www.pfdf.org

The Collaboration Challenge

How Nonprofits and Businesses
Succeed Through Strategic Alliances

James E. Austin
Harvard Business School

Foreword by Frances Hesselbein
and John C. Whitehead

Jossey-Bass Publishers
San Francisco

Jossey-Bass books and products are available through most bookstores. To contact Jossey-Bass directly, call (888) 378-2537, fax to (800) 605-2665, or visit our website at www.josseybass.com.

Substantial discounts on bulk quantities of Jossey-Bass books are available to corporations, professional associations, and other organizations. For details and discount information, contact the special sales department at Jossey-Bass.

Manufactured in the United States of America on Lyons Falls Turin Book. This paper is acid-free and 100 percent totally chlorine-free.

Library of Congress Cataloging-in-Publication Data

Austin, James E.
　　The collaboration challenge : how nonprofits and businesses succeed through strategic alliances / James E. Austin.
　　　　p. cm.
　　Includes bibliographical references and index.
　　ISBN 0-7879-5220-6 (alk. paper)
　　1. Strategic alliances (Business)　2. Strategic planning.　3. Industrial management.
4. Nonprofit organization—Management.　I. Title.

HD69.S8 A94 2000
658'.044—dc21
　　　　　　　　　　　　　　　　　　　　　　　　　　　　　　　　　　　　99-088237

HB Printing　10 9 8 7 6 5 4 3 2 1　　　　　　　　　　　　　FIRST EDITION

Contents

Foreword

We are living in a time when no organization can succeed on its own. The development of results-focused nonprofits and businesses creates a growing opportunity for these organizations to work together and create new possibilities that further their respective missions. Nonprofits know they must become more businesslike. Businesses know they must become more socially responsible. A growing number of farsighted leaders are moving their organizations beyond the institutional barriers to cooperation and are meeting the collaboration challenge head-on. These leaders are not content to limit their vision of what can be achieved to the results within their own enterprise. They count on the results made possible by the combined efforts of effective organizations across all sectors of the economy.

These are the leaders we meet in this important new book by the Harvard Business School's James Austin: people such as Howard Schultz, chairman and CEO of Starbucks, and Peter Bell, president of CARE, who forged a partnership that continues to improve the lives of farmers around the world—and brings unexpected benefits to both organizations at home. And people such as The Nature Conservancy's president John Sawhill and Georgia-Pacific's CEO Pete Correll, who discovered that traditional adversaries can find ways to work together for the common good.

Jim Austin takes us deep inside thriving partnerships engineered by successful businesses such as Hewlett-Packard, Reebok, the Bayer

Corporation, Timberland, Nordstrom, and Visa and respected non-profit organizations such as Amnesty International, City Year, National Geographic, American Humane Association, and Time to Read. We discover that collaborations between businesses and community groups and other nonprofits can bring benefits far beyond the tangible objectives they were designed to accomplish. Well-managed collaborations can help build brand identity and goodwill, reinforce employee commitment, and uncover new business opportunities and sources of revenue. And—essential in this knowledge society—they provide powerful opportunities for organizational learning.

Of course the key to achieving such benefits is to understand the nature of collaboration, the potential pitfalls, the points for leverage, and the management strategies that work in bringing different organizations together. That is the reason Jim Austin wrote this book. He has studied a wide variety of partnerships and collaborations in all kinds of industries, from low-tech to high-tech, and involving all kinds of nonprofits, from local grassroots organizations to global giants with household names. He gained unprecedented access to the decision makers who instituted and managed these alliances and who provide firsthand accounts of their successes, trials, and lessons learned. Sifting through these myriad alliances, Austin has uncovered the common elements and key strategies that make for effective collaborations. In *The Collaboration Challenge*, he illuminates these key lessons for all leaders, and makes it possible for each of us to meet the collaboration challenge.

We are pleased to collaborate on the Foreword to Jim Austin's important new book. Through our work with the Initiative on Social Enterprise at the Harvard Business School and the Drucker Foundation, we have both been traveling on parallel tracks. This book links the engines of our organizations to pull toward a common goal: enhancing the leadership and management capabilities of nonprofits. The Drucker Foundation is pleased to present this practical and inspiring guide to the collaborations essential to building a better world in the times to come.

As we look around us in a new century, we realize that businesses and nonprofits in today's interconnected world will neither thrive nor survive with visions confined within the walls of their own organizations. They need to look beyond the walls and find partners who can help achieve greater results and build the vital communities to meet the challenges ahead. That is why *The Collaboration Challenge* is so important to all leaders, whether in business, government, or nonprofit institutions.

December 1999   Frances Hesselbein
                                   Chairman
                                   Board of Governors
                                   The Peter F. Drucker Foundation
                                   for Nonprofit Management

                                   John C. Whitehead
                                   Founder
                                   The John C. Whitehead Fund
                                   for Not-for-Profit Management,
                                   Harvard Business School

Preface

This book is for nonprofit and business leaders who are seeking ways to partner effectively with each other for mutual benefit and social good. Cross-sector collaboration between nonprofits and businesses has been growing, and this trend will accelerate as we enter this new century. These alliances are becoming of strategic importance to the partners. Yet there is a relative paucity of literature on this phenomenon.

This book documents the experience of over fifteen strategic alliances between business and nonprofit organizations and establishes a basis for understanding the nature and evolution of cross-sector collaborations. It presents an analytical framework leaders and others can use to think systematically about creating, building, and managing such partnerships so as to generate value for both partners and for society. By conducting in-depth analyses of partnering experiences, I have attempted to capture the wisdom of the practitioners and present insights on the determinants of alliance effectiveness. Readers will discover new ways of looking at cross-sector collaborations and practical guidance on how to achieve successful alliances.

The Audience

This book offers many useful tools and insights not only for executives and directors of business and nonprofit organizations engaging in strategic partnerships but also for staff, line managers, and consultants who carry some responsibility for planning and implementing these partnerships. Academics and graduate students in both business and nonprofit management will also find innovative ideas to reflect on in these pages.

Overview of the Contents

Chapter One introduces the major alliances discussed in the book and the many forces impelling them, making the new century an age of alliances for many businesses and nonprofits.

The next five chapters analyze how these alliances function, with many case study examples. Chapter Two looks at the various stages a business-nonprofit partnership may pass through, with different needs and benefits for the parties. Chapter Three addresses getting started, particularly at the top leadership level. Partnerships between businesses and nonprofits, just like partnerships between businesses alone, must be built around a strategic fit. Chapter Four explores the important areas of alignment, and Chapter Five describes how partners can analyze the value of their collaboration. Chapter Six discusses the ongoing practical management of a partnership.

Chapter Seven offers a detailed case study that demonstrates at length the drivers and enablers of alliances discussed in the previous chapters.

Finally, Chapter Eight presents a series of highly practical collaboration guidelines and a list of key questions for leaders.

Acknowledgments

I would like to express my deep appreciation to Harvard Business School (HBS) research associates Linda Carrigan and Arthur McCaffrey for their excellent assistance in the research project that underlies this book. Their diligence and skill in carrying out case study fieldwork and writing up the results were outstanding and their intellectual companionship invaluable. I am also grateful to Katherine Korman Frey, Harvard Business School M.B.A., 1999, for her energetic and enthusiastic assistance in conducting the survey component of the research.

I am particularly grateful to the businesses and the nonprofit organizations studied in this research project for their generosity in sharing their time, wisdom, and experience so that others might learn. Their community spirit is exemplary. It is my hope that this book they have helped to create will also prove useful in furthering their cross-sector collaborations.

The manuscript for this book benefited from the insightful review of my colleague Professor Rosabeth Moss Kanter, whose pioneering studies of alliances guided many of us who have followed in her footsteps. The original research was presented at the Harvard Business School Social Enterprise Research Forum in November 1998, and the comments of the forum's academic and practitioner participants also enriched this book. I especially appreciate the helpful suggestions of my HBS colleagues Allen Grossman, Bloomberg Senior Lecturer in Philanthropy, and Elaine Backman, senior research associate. Alan Shrader, Jossey-Bass executive editor, was a gifted adviser as I sought clarity and utility for the reader. The manuscript also benefited from John Simon's and Elspeth MacHattie's skilled editorial assistance.

I am also grateful to Frances Hesselbein, chairman, and Rob Johnston, senior vice president, of the Drucker Foundation for the opportunity to publish this book as part of the foundation's distinguished book series. I first presented these concepts about alliances at a Drucker Foundation annual leadership conference. Peter Drucker's vision and wisdom have served as an inspiration and a magnet, drawing many of us through new intellectual doors that he opened. It is my hope that this book contributes to the unrelenting quest for learning and excellence embodied by Peter Drucker and the Drucker Foundation.

Finally, this book would not have been possible without the support of the Harvard Business School Division of Research and HBS dean Kim Clark's encouragement of the Initiative on Social Enterprise.

Boston, Massachussetts   James E. Austin
December 1999

To John McArthur

*former dean of the Harvard Business School
and extraordinary educational entrepreneur*

and John Whitehead

*distinguished investment banker, government policymaker,
and nonprofit director*

Their vision of the profound role of leadership and management education in the betterment of society gave birth to the Harvard Business School Initiative on Social Enterprise. Leaders of action create lasting legacies. This book is one part of the legacy from their vibrant and enduring social enterprise leadership.

The Collaboration
Challenge

The Strategic Benefits of Alliances

The twenty-first century will be the *age of alliances*. In this age, collaboration between nonprofit organizations and corporations will grow in frequency and strategic importance. Collaborative relationships will increasingly migrate from the traditionally philanthropic, characterized by benevolent donor and grateful recipient, toward deeper, strategic alliances. These changes are already under way, and the changing alliance landscape is rich in variety, with businesses and nonprofits from Boston to Seattle finding new ways to work together to achieve their goals and contribute to society.

The Faces of Collaboration

These alliances do not require grandiose strategic plans; patience and perseverance are often sufficient to turn small beginnings into significant strategic alliances. Consider, for example, the relationship between the nonprofit City Year and the outdoor boot and apparel outfitter Timberland, begun in 1989 when City Year requested from Timberland fifty pairs of boots for its urban youth service corps, founded the previous year. The service corps program organizes youths from diverse ethnic, racial, and economic backgrounds into teams to work on a wide range of community service projects such as serving as classroom aides in inner-city schools or assisting staff at neighborhood Boys and Girls Clubs. Expansion of the relationship over the ensuing decade found Timberland supplying City Year's official uniform and becoming its major corporate backer, providing about $1 million annually in cash and in-kind gifts and helping the organization to expand nationally. City Year in turn played a central role in helping Timberland develop and implement its strategy for community service and a high-engagement corporate culture. City Year also helped Timberland employees carry out community service projects, to which they gave more than twenty thousand employee hours in 1998. Each organization considers the relationship with the other to be of central strategic importance.

That these emerging strategic alliances go far beyond check writing in order to leverage the competencies of each partner and create two-way value is evidenced by, among others, the collaboration between The College Fund (UNCF) and Merck. UNCF, the largest and oldest minority educational assistance organization in the United States, and Merck, a leading global pharmaceutical company, have been collaborating for three years to increase the number of African American biologists and chemists. In 1995, they launched the UNCF-Merck Science Internships. The undergraduates, doctoral students, and postdoctoral scientists who receive these internships are assigned mentors from Merck's research staff and given assignments at Merck's research facilities. Through its network of associated colleges, UNCF affords Merck access to bright minority students with an interest in science, and these students are in turn provided access to Merck's scientific talent, facilities, and work opportunities.

Similarly, the National Science Resources Center (NSRC), a nonprofit organization created by the Smithsonian Institution and National Academy of Sciences to improve the teaching of science in K–12 education, has brought to a collaboration with Hewlett-Packard (HP) high credibility and access to key curriculum decision makers in the public education system. A leading designer, manufacturer, and service provider of products and systems for measurement, computation, and communications, HP, like Merck, has a basic interest in increasing the supply of scientists. NSRC has focused on curriculum design and teacher training. HP's technical advice and the active involvement of its scientists and managers have lent a valuable perspective and competency that NSRC alone was unable to bring to the educational and developmental processes. Through this alliance, HP has enhanced its reputation in the educational community, and participating employees have enjoyed highly motivating and satisfying experiences.

Businesses and nonprofits sometimes perceive a natural strategic fit—the mutuality of interests that is central to creating strong alliances—such as the fit between the American Humane Association (AHA) and Ralston Purina Company. It was logical for the AHA, which advocates for animal causes and represents animal shelters throughout the nation, and Ralston Purina, the world's largest producer of pet foods, to join forces to create the Pets for People program, which aims to increase pet adoptions and thereby save thousands of animals that would otherwise have been euthanized for lack of homes.

A common objective, in this case the promotion of literacy, is also the basis of a strong collaboration between the Time to Read national program and media and entertainment giant Time Warner, Inc. Time to Read helps local nonprofits such as Chicago's Off the Street Club recruit children, youths, and even adults from disadvantaged areas for tutoring by Time Warner employee volunteers trained by Time to Read. Instead of financial grants, Time Warner supplies reading materials (especially magazines published by the company), classroom space, and tutors at its various offices around the country.

Even when a strategic fit is not immediately obvious, common ground can often be discovered. The alliance between The Nature Conservancy and Georgia-Pacific involved a dramatic shift from a contentious to a collaborative relationship. Historically, The Nature Conservancy (TNC), an international conservation organization and the largest private owner of nature preserves in the United States, and Georgia-Pacific Corporation, one of the world's largest forest products companies, had pursued competing agendas for common lands. The former wanted to preserve the land untouched, the latter to use it intensively. However, mounting environmental pressures on the forestry industry and growing difficulties for environmentalists in gaining control of ecosystems through land purchases led these organizations to reassess their opposing strategies. Their 1994 landmark agreement to jointly manage unique forested wetlands in North Carolina represented a substantial shift for both organizations to strategies built on partnerships to accomplish both their individual and their newly shared goals.

A similar incongruity seemed to exist between Reading Is Fundamental (RIF) and Visa International. RIF is a national nonprofit that works through local volunteer programs in thousands of communities throughout the United States to inspire young people to read. Visa operates the world's leading consumer credit card payment system. Although there is no obvious connection between the credit card business and literacy promotion, research that revealed that this social cause was viewed positively by Visa cardholders became the basis for a cause-related marketing collaboration in which Visa donates to RIF a percentage of charges during certain periods when the reading program is promoted.

Another unexpected fit is that between the human rights advocacy organization Amnesty International and sports shoe manufacturer Reebok International Ltd. Reebok's CEO, seeing a connection between the cause of human rights and the underlying values that he wanted to foster in Reebok's corporate culture, sponsored a celebrity concert world tour that Amnesty International had organized to promote the fortieth anniversary of the Universal Declaration of Human Rights. Reebok has since engaged in other activities with Amnesty International, and human rights has become a core value in the company.

Before strategic fit can be explored, a potential partner must be found. That task can be particularly daunting when cross-sector alliances are sought because information about the availability and suitability of partners is not readily available. Sometimes serendipity appears to play a role. The idea of forming an alliance with Starbucks Corporation came to a CARE manager as he was drinking a cup of Starbucks coffee. A systematic getting-acquainted process began formally in 1991, when Starbucks was a young, $20 million coffee retailer and CARE was a well-known, forty-five-year-old international relief and development institution with annual revenues of approximately $300 million, some ten thousand employees, and operations throughout the world, and it evolved into an increasingly deep partnership. By 1998, Starbucks had boomed into a global company with sales of almost $1 billion and was CARE's largest corporate donor. CARE president Peter Bell has referred to the alliance as "having more richness to it than other relationships."[1] And Starbucks chairman and CEO Howard Schultz illustrated the importance of the partnership to Starbucks when he said: "We have to weigh what's affordable against what we think is right. That's why we keep giving to CARE even when profits are tight."[2]

Alliances can take many different forms. Some, such as the arrangement between the Bidwell Training Center and the Bayer Corporation, come to involve multiple partners in an effort to assemble more abundant resources and more powerful combinations of competencies. Bidwell, which trains disadvantaged inner-city youths and unemployed adults of southwestern Pennsylvania for jobs in high-tech, culinary, and medical fields, partnered with Bayer, a major pharmaceutical and chemical company, to develop a chemical technician training program. Then the two partners incorporated other chemical companies and government actors into the alliance in order to bring in more capabilities and resources and expand job placement opportunities.

Similarly, MCI WorldCom, a major communications technology company, has partnered with the National Geographic Society to create the MarcoPolo geography Web site to promote Internet content integration in the K-12 curriculum and is simultaneously partnering with the National Endowment for the Humanities, the Council of Great City Schools, National Council on Economic Education, National Council of Teachers of Mathematics, and the American Association for the Advancement of Science to create analogous Web sites in other disciplines. The resulting coalition creates an educational program that none of the partners could have developed alone.

Family-owned businesses also engage in cross-sector alliances, as illustrated by the relationship between the Jimmy Fund and the Perini Corporation. Initiated in 1948 by Louis Perini, second-generation CEO of a family-owned, Boston-based construction company, and Sidney Farber, M.D., a pioneer in cancer treatment, this collaboration came to include the then–league champion Boston baseball team,[3] also owned by Perini at that time. The team became a major sponsor of the Jimmy Fund, helping raise money for the treatment of children with cancer. Although the Jimmy Fund has mobilized a multitude of other major support sources, its partnership with the Perini family, the family corporation, and the Boston Red Sox continues to this day.

Nordstrom, a leading clothing retailer predominantly owned and run by the Nordstrom family and headquartered in Seattle, was an early and major supporter of its local United Way, the seventh largest in the United States. The two organizations interact in a variety of ways, including serving as mutual technical advisers. Thus even the United Way, among the most well established, traditional philanthropic vehicles, is also engaging in strategic alliances that encompass much more than a check-writing relationship.

These and the other alliances researched for this book reveal considerable diversity in the types of businesses and social sector organizations involved and in their forms of collaboration. Each of the alliances that we visit in the subsequent chapters has distinctive characteristics, yet their collective experiences yield important lessons about the dynamics, management, and payoffs from strategic cross-sector collaboration.

The Collaboration Imperative

Cross-sector collaboration is clearly occurring, but why? First, at the macro level of the larger society, various forces are creating an environment that strongly encourages collaboration. Second, at the micro level of the institutions, there are a multitude of positive payoffs from partnering.

Macro-Level Forces

The imperative for collaboration stems from the rapid, structural, and probably irreversible changes being generated by powerful political, economic, and social forces.

Political Forces

In the wake of a major rethinking of the role and size of the federal government, the era of ever-bigger national government is coming to an end. No longer can society look to the federal government as the main problem solver. Trust in government and politicians has diminished; the limits of the state have been acknowledged. This has triggered a massive devolution of social functions from the federal to local levels and from the public to the private sector. The Reagan, Bush, and Clinton administrations have all urged corporations and nonprofit organizations to assume a greater role in solving society's problems. This shifting of responsibilities is greatly increasing the demands on the nonprofit and business sectors and pushing them toward collaboration.

Economic Forces

The political mandate for fiscal austerity and a balanced budget slashed the traditional federal funding of many nonprofit organizations (NPOs). The federal government has been the biggest funder of many segments of the nonprofit sector, and NPOs have been proliferating rapidly over the past fifteen years. So we have more nonprofits chasing increasingly limited federal economic resources. Although some social sectors have seen greater government funding as the strong economy has produced budget surpluses, vast numbers of NPOs feel severely underfunded in proportion to their missions. They view collaboration as a means of economizing on scarce resources and tapping new sources of assistance.

Social Forces

Finally, the magnitude and complexity of our social and economic problems are growing, and these problems are now outstripping the institutional and economic capabilities of individual nonprofit and business organizations to deal with them. As the commons grows more complicated and the identity of the keepers becomes less clear, collaboration has emerged as the new mandate.

Benefits of Partnering for Nonprofits

The macro forces are creating an environment in which collaboration is becoming the rule rather than the exception for NPOs. As economic imperatives call for rationalization in the nonprofit industry, many nonprofits, like their for-profit counterparts, will need to restructure and downsize in order to remain viable. An integral part of this strategic process should be a dispassionate analysis of the feasibility of continuing to operate independently. Going it alone is quickly moving to the endangered strategy list. The collaboration supplanting it is taking place both between NPOs and between NPOs and businesses. Among the benefits to be realized by nonprofits from this partnering are cost savings, economies of scale and scope, synergies, and revenue enhancement.

Cost Savings

Many nonprofits will be propelled into *austerity alliances* with other NPOs. Created in response to financial imperatives, these cost-cutting collaborations are intended to eliminate duplicative costs and excess capacity through shared facilities, services, or activities. For example, The Children's Trust Fund and the United Way of South Carolina combined boards, staff, and offices to economize on facilities cost, payroll, and volunteer time and to magnify the impact of their similar operations.[4] Austerity has been a particularly powerful mechanism for responding to the growing cost reduction pressures in the health care field. Three medium-size nonprofit hospitals in a Chicago suburb created a jointly owned nonprofit to acquire and operate a magnetic resonance imaging facility, for example, thereby reducing their capital outlays for equipment that purchased and operated individually would have gone underused.[5] The economic imperative of consolidation has also driven mergers between nonprofit and for-profit hospitals. The primary benefit that organizations receive from these austerity alliances is economizing on scarce resources. NPO-business collaborations are generally not austerity oriented but sometimes efficiency is enhanced.

Economies of Scale and Scope

Other economically driven alliances between nonprofits aim to achieve economies of scale or scope. These alliances combine or extend similar organizations' markets, client bases, or purchased inputs. Economies of scale are realized from the resulting volume increases. These savings-oriented alliances also expand the partners' visibility and sphere of impact, potentially improving image or credibility. Collaborations that bring different types of services together for an existing client base may result in a more efficient delivery system. Enhanced breadth of services can increase convenience and utility for, and thus attract more, clients, increasing the use of the combined facilities. The Denver-based Osage Initiatives Project, for example, brought together in a single center five nonprofits that provide distinct services to low-income and welfare recipients. These entities, though still autonomous, have created a collaborative one-stop assistance center that offers literacy training and GED preparation, affordable housing location, office skills development, and financing for new businesses. The shared facility has enabled these NPOs not only to economize but also to deliver more services to their common clients.[6]

Some collaborations between NPOs and businesses have enabled the nonprofit to scale up from a local to a nationwide operation. This also creates economies of scale and magnifies impact.

Synergies

Nonprofits also realize synergies from collaborations that bring together two or more organizations' complementary capabilities. Organizations, whether nonprofits, for-profits, or governments, with complementary capabilities are able to accomplish more together than they can separately. A related type of collaboration centers on *inescapable interdependence*, the concept that no single entity has all the inputs necessary to address an identified social need effectively. When you cannot go it alone and succeed, collaboration becomes a prerequisite to effectiveness. Still other alliances center around creating a *critical mass*—the cooperating groups do not necessarily bring different resources to the table but they do share a common concern about the particular problem. They come together to assemble sufficient collective confidence, knowledge, financial resources, or political power to enable them to be effective.

Revenue Enhancement

It is clear that various benefits push or pull nonprofits into collaborations with different types of partners. Their collaborations with businesses have traditionally been viewed primarily as fundraising relationships, the benefit being revenue generation, often with relatively few restrictions on use. The changing environment suggests a need for a broader, more strategic view of resource combinations on the part of corporations and nonprofits alike.

Benefits of Partnering for Corporations

The surveys, interviews, and company studies my colleagues and I conducted reveal that business executives perceive cross-sector collaborations to yield important benefits in four areas: strategy enrichment, human resource management, culture building, and business generation.

Strategy Enrichment

Corporate giving to NPOs is a part of most major companies' strategies. This philanthropy has been increasing in real terms since the late 1980s and has been growing faster than foundation or individual giving. Although corporate charity has not grown as fast as profits, by 1998 it had passed the $8 billion mark.[7] But leading companies have been reformulating their traditional check-writing approach to philanthropy, choosing a broader, more strategic engagement with their communities.[8] For example, Citicorp, a global financial services corporation, has made community service an integral part of its new worldwide corporate strategy and one of six key areas on which it measures company performance (the others are people management, customer/franchise performance, strategic cost management, risk and control, and financial performance).[9] Managers' contributions to community betterment are explicitly assessed through Citicorp's balanced scorecard accountability system.

Citicorp's strategy is to be an "embedded" corporation, an integral part of the institutional fabric, in each of the communities in which it operates. This means achieving a level of involvement that extends well beyond offering services in the financial marketplace to include "assessing the impact of business decisions on the community and mitigating any negative consequences, and engaging in activities—volunteer and philanthropic—that help build the community." Citicorp's management has described the rationale for this strategic engagement in this way: "We do this because it is the right thing to do and can offer profitable business opportunities. We also do this because we want a positive and trusted image with customers, potential customers, regulators, legislators, and community groups, all of which supports our global image as a trusted brand name. We are talking here about how we run our business, not just about contributions, volunteerism and PR. . . . It has moved from 'nice to do' to 'need to do' as part of our business strategy."

It is myopic to think of a corporation's community engagement strategy simply and narrowly as altruism. Such a strategy also makes good business sense, according to former chairman of Goldman Sachs John Whitehead, who remarked: "Don't think that this is some kind of charitable thing where you will get rewarded in heaven. You get rewarded right away because you'll be known as a company that is conscious of its social responsibility; you'll attract better quality employees; your stock will sell at a higher multiple; and all sorts of good things will come of it." Professors Sandra Waddock and Samuel Graves's recent rigorous analysis of the Standard and Poors 500 companies revealed that strong corporate social performance, including community service, resulted in a "virtuous circle,"[10] both benefiting from and contributing to strong financial performance. In effect, corporate strategy can be significantly enriched by incorporating meaningful community engagement through collaboration with NPOs.

Human Resource Management

Community involvement is an attraction to potential employees and a competitive advantage in tight professional labor markets. A Conference Board survey of 454 companies revealed that 90 percent of managers believed that their companies' community volunteer programs helped these companies attract better employees.[11] Company support for community service activities also enhances employee motivation and morale, thereby strengthening company loyalty and retention. A study of 188 companies found employee morale to be three times higher in firms heavily involved in their communities.[12] Working with nonprofits is also perceived to benefit junior and senior managers developmentally by expanding their opportunities to practice management and leadership, broadening their perspectives through interaction with different types of individuals, enhancing their core capabilities such as planning and teamwork, and teaching them collaborative leadership. Employee involvement in community service can also illuminate individuals' capabilities, values, and attitudes, allowing the company to conduct more accurate employee assessments.

Culture Building

For many companies, community service is now becoming a more integral part of corporate culture. In farsighted companies, especially, it is viewed not as an add-on but as a central force that shapes and reinforces the core values that elicit employee behavior vital to the success of the business. Community service can foster empathy and caring, attitudes that reinforce a service-oriented mentality. It can encourage high-involvement and high-impact leadership behavior by reinforcing active engagement aimed at making a difference. During a crisis it can serve as organizational glue, creating cohesion through common values. Finally, it can serve as a compatibility checkpoint when a company needs to assess values congruency with potential business partners.

Business Generation

Businesses can also benefit from the external linkages they develop through or as a consequence of community service. Although managers report that community service activities are undertaken primarily to make a social contribution, they are also widely agreed that these activities can generate business as well by enhancing a company's reputation; building goodwill; expanding networks, relationships, and markets; increasing access to key consumer groups; and providing an arena for testing innovations. This view lends credence to the assertion that doing good is good business.[13]

The Cross-Sector Partnering Difference

Corporate involvement in the social sector almost always entails some form of collaboration with nonprofits. Although many of the key success factors and challenges of cross-sector collaboration are also found in intrasectoral (that is, corporation-to-corporation or nonprofit-to-nonprofit) alliances,[14] the respondents in my research indicated that cross-sector partnering was distinctive because the participants in any such alliance were likely to have noticeably different performance measures, competitive dynamics, organization cultures, decision-making styles, personnel competencies, professional languages, incentive and motivational structures, and emotional content.

Both City Year and Timberland executives, for example, believed the potential and process for value creation in corporation-nonprofit alliances to be different from the potential and process in same-sector collaborations. Observed City Year cofounder Michael Brown, "We tend to look at a for-profit as a place to connect a million dots. And we tend to work with nonprofits to connect to one or two dots. The corporations have many more access points." Added City Year's other founder, Alan Khazei, "One of the things that inhibit partnerships between nonprofits is the fear of splitting a limited pie." Timberland COO Jeffrey Swartz made this distinction: "It's much easier to start a relationship with another business. We know why we are there. We start fast and then it slows down. With a nonprofit you start slow. There is a real suspicion on both sides of the agenda. But once we got past that original hump, the relationship [with City Year] has gone much deeper and further." "The hardest challenge," explained an MCI WorldCom executive, "is the cultural differences between corporate and nonprofit organizations. We just move much faster. Negotiations are different. Accountability is different. Everything is different. Once you understand how nonprofits work, think, and operate, you can get a lot of great things accomplished. Companies just need to take the time to develop a relationship in full." We can see that these differences create distinctive challenges, but also great opportunities.

Collaboration across sectors is clearly not achieved by simply applying standard operating procedures for collaborating with peer organizations. NPOs and businesses need to adapt their relationship-building approaches to the special nature of cross-sector alliances. As they do so, they will find it useful to take a strategic perspective.

The Strategic Perspective

Alliances are vehicles for achieving each participant's mission, so partnering should be considered an integral part of any NPO's or company's strategy. Any organization must think strategically to get the most out of cross-sector collaborations. For each alliance it must delineate systematically the why, what, whom, when, and how of creating, developing, and managing the relationship, answering the following strategic questions.

Why should we collaborate? The organization should specify the function and value of collaboration in terms of where the collaboration fits into the organization's overall strategy and how it contributes to the accomplishment of its mission.

What type of collaboration should we undertake? Given the multitude of collaboration modalities, the organization must understand the implications of these different modes in order to select the optimum one for each specific circumstance.

With whom should we collaborate? To select the right partner, the organization must find the right fit between missions, values, needs, and competencies.

When should we collaborate? Timing is an integral ingredient of strategy formulation. The organization must take as central concerns deciding when to embark upon an alliance and when to change its nature.

How should we collaborate? The organization must view the specific design and management of an alliance as part of an ongoing iterative process that evolves with the collaboration.

The key considerations for companies and NPOs as they work on these questions are embedded in the analyses presented in subsequent chapters. The knowledge that must underlie all these considerations, however, is an understanding of the basic process of creating and developing cross-sector alliances.

Alliance Creation and Development

The alliance creation and development process comprises five main elements, each of which is elaborated throughout the following five chapters by means of multiple and rich examples and lessons from many strategic alliances.

1. *Understanding strategic collaboration.* An important starting point for thinking strategically about cross-sector collaborations is to recognize that relationships may pass through different stages. Chapter Two presents a framework, the Collaboration Continuum, that reveals these stages and helps partners understand the types of alliance they have developed or might want to develop. This chapter also emphasizes the importance of recognizing the changing nature, requisites, and benefits of alliances as they move along the continuum.

2. *Making the connection.* The starting point in alliance building, finding a potential partner, is complicated by the nature of what I term the alliance marketplace. Chapter Three examines some

problems associated with this marketplace, in particular the barriers to connecting and the subsequent tasks of becoming acquainted, engaging top leadership, and creating personal connections with the cause and between partners.

3. *Ensuring strategic fit.* Having found and gotten to know one another, potential partners need to focus on strategic fit. The closer the fit, the stronger the alliance. I explore in Chapter Four the vital task of discovering and developing areas of alignment between organizations' missions, strategies, and values.

4. *Generating value.* The sustainability of an alliance depends fundamentally on the value of the collaboration to each partner and to society, yet value is often the least well examined aspect of cross-sector collaboration. Chapter Five sets forth a four-part framework that facilitates systematic analysis of the tasks of defining, creating, balancing, and renewing the value of alliances to their participants.

5. *Managing the relationship.* How well an alliance is executed ultimately determines whether its potential value is realized. Chapter Six deals with the critical tasks of making the partnership work through organization, communication, trust-building, accountability, and learning and through the strategic management of a collaboration portfolio.

Through a full case study of a single strategic alliance, Chapter Seven illustrates and integrates the concepts presented in the previous chapters, identifying key drivers and enablers of the alliance. Chapter Eight synthesizes a set of collaboration guidelines from the research and insights.

Throughout this book I have made a special effort to impart, in their own voices, the wisdom of nonprofit and business managers engaged in strategic alliances. Embedded in their words are powerful insights and lessons about how to effectively meet the collaboration challenge. In the following pages, the world of practice is our classroom.[15]

2

Understanding Strategic Collaboration

Do you know what type of cross-sector collaborative relationship your organization has or wants? In the absence of a ready typology of collaborations, you may find this question difficult to answer. In the business world, strategic frameworks abound, and new ones emerge with great frequency in the business world. This is not merely technical faddism; such frameworks usually emerge from empirical scrutiny of what businesses are doing and managers are thinking. Insofar as a conceptual framework represents a distillation of the complexity of practice, it can be particularly useful to managers, helping them see complex phenomena more clearly and think more systematically about strategic paths and choices.

A framework that enables managers to envision different collaboration options is essential if they are to think strategically about cross-sector alliances. Such a framework must recognize that strategic alliances are multifaceted relationships that change over time. How they change depends largely on the strategic choices the partners make. The framework discussed in this chapter is based on my research into cross-sector alliances. It allows partners to categorize their collaborations, to understand how these collaborations might evolve over time, and to analyze the resulting changes in the nature, requisites, and importance of their collaborative relationships. Managers with such an understanding will be able to make more informed choices about their partnering strategies.

I label this framework the Collaboration Continuum. This chapter elaborates the continuum and defines, with the aid of detailed examples, the three stages through which collaborations can pass. It then discusses the use of the framework as a strategic tool.

The Collaboration Continuum

It was the recognition that cross-sector relationships come in many forms and evolve over time that led me to characterize the degree and form of interaction between nonprofits and corporations as the Collaboration Continuum. I term the three stages through which a relationship may pass *philanthropic, transactional,* and *integrative.* As you read about these stages, try to determine where on the continuum your cross-sector collaborations fall.

Philanthropic Stage

In the philanthropic stage the nature of the relationship between corporation and nonprofit is largely that of charitable donor and recipient. Such relationships are the most commonplace, but increasingly they are migrating to the next stage. In the philanthropic stage the engagement between organizations is generally limited to an annual solicitation from an NPO that elicits a donation from a corporation. These financial resources may be significant to the NPO but are generally not economically critical to either party. Such a collaboration, generally being limited to submitting a grant proposal and gratefully acknowledging the subsequent donation, is relatively simple to administer and not deemed particularly important to either organization's mission. Follow-up reports on funds usage or impact are minimal. In lieu of making a specific grant request, an NPO might sell corporate donors tickets to a fundraising event such as a dinner. In the philanthropic relationship each side benefits modestly. The NPO increases its funding; the company enhances its reputation as a community supporter.

To illustrate, I return to the initial relationship between City Year and Timberland. The first contact between the two organizations took the form of a cold call made in 1989 by a City Year fundraiser who was particularly skilled at obtaining in-kind donations. She asked Timberland for fifty pairs of boots, to be part of the uniform for City Year's youth corps, which had completed a pilot summer project and was expanding into a year-long community service engagement. Approved by a Timberland administrative assistant, the request at this stage amounted to nothing more than a minor charitable gift. The next year City Year requested and received seventy pairs of boots. Recalled City Year cofounder Michael Brown: "This was now a two-year-old relationship with two conversations, two faxes, and a feeling a little bit like, 'OK, they just did that, send a thank-you, but don't bother them.'" Timberland COO Jeffrey Swartz described the interaction as traditional charitable giving, a reaction to a supplicant's request: "Our expectation was a thank-you note and a small sense of self-congratulation and nothing more."

Collaboration in the philanthropic stage is highly circumscribed in terms of resources deployed and points of interaction. Timberland's relationship with City Year was incidental to Timberland's mission; it was somewhat more important to City Year but not critical. Few individuals and none of the top leadership were involved. The benefit equation was simple: City Year secured an in-kind donation, enhanced in value by virtue of the boots being deemed the best available, and this donation set a quality standard for the uniform that would ultimately be important to City Year's identity. Timberland received good feelings, or in Swartz's words: "[City Year does] good deeds, and we would like to feel better about our corporate mission personally and collectively; we are lucky that things are going our way this particular moment, so we can afford to send some boots and feel good about ourselves. It wasn't a request for a check. It was a request for Timberland boots, and so it spoke to what we do and who we are. It felt nice to be valued for who you are."

At this early stage traditional mind-sets constrained the relationship. City Year operated with a fundraising mentality and suffered from what Michael Brown referred to as the *gratefulness syndrome*: its task was to extract resources and, if successful, graciously issue thanks but not "bother" the donor thereafter. On the corporate side Timberland was constrained by the *charity syndrome*: give to good causes that solicit assistance but deal with these donations as a peripheral part of your activities and minimize your time investment. On both sides, minimizing interaction and communication was the mode of operation. Although the company did perceive some psychological benefits, the value flow was largely one-way, with the corporation making an in-kind donation and the nonprofit being the beneficiary. Expectations and investments were relatively low and narrowly defined on both sides. Such low-level engagements between nonprofits and companies are commonplace and often long-standing, their mutual benefits real and not insignificant. But increasingly such relationships, including that of City Year and Timberland, migrate to the next relationship stage.

Transactional Stage

In the transactional stage, organizations carry out their resource exchanges through specific activities, such as cause-related marketing, event sponsorships, licensing, and paid service arrangements. Engagement of the partners is more active at this stage and the value flow more significantly two-way. For corporations, in particular, the relationship begins to connect more directly with business operations. Cause-related marketing and event sponsorships are generally handled by the marketing rather than the corporate philanthropy staff. These activities represent the fastest growing marketing expenditure category, pumping around a half-billion dollars into NPO collaborators.[1] Many of these collaborations are the participants' initial relationship and are not preceded by a philanthropic stage relationship.

Although collaboration in the transactional stage may focus on the *deal* between the partners and involve sharply circumscribed transactions such as those just listed, often it includes other important resource exchanges as well. This is particularly true when the relationship has evolved from the philanthropic stage. Company employee volunteer programs often emerge as extensions of financial donations made to NPOs in the philanthropic stage of an alliance, and this involvement of company personnel begins to generate many of the employee motivational and developmental benefits mentioned in the previous chapter. Organizations may also exchange expertise in other ways. Interaction between the partners broadens and intensifies. Strategic fit becomes closer. The complexity of the alliance grows, and the nature and magnitude of the benefits also multiply.

To view the second stage on the Collaboration Continuum more closely, let's turn again to the evolution of the City Year and Timberland alliance. The door to the second stage was opened by City Year cofounder Alan Khazei when he visited Timberland with the idea of getting to know the company better. Khazei and the City Year development officer combined a City Year staff outing in New Hampshire with a previously arranged meeting with Jeff Swartz and the Timberland vice president of marketing (and subsequently vice president of social enterprise), Ken Freitas, at Timberland's nearby headquarters. This meeting was pivotal in opening up new collaboration possibilities by increasing each side's understanding of the other's vision. Recounted Swartz: "When Alan came by Timberland to say thanks for the boots, I said to him, 'You are out there actually saving lives. I am making boots, but I have always wanted to save lives.' And Alan said, 'Let me show you how they can be related.' His message was, 'Through City Year it's going to be okay to do what you dream and dare. We will provide you with a vehicle for your beliefs.'" Freitas added: "The meeting was important because for the first time we realized that there was more here than a typical charitable donation. There was a real connection. The similarities between what each organization wanted to do and how it wanted to achieve its vision were striking." The partners' interaction and dialogue enabled them to discover that their missions overlapped and that they could create new value from collaboration.

A transactional stage relationship is mutually beneficial; it has two-way benefit flows that participants consciously seek and identify. As Swartz defined it: "We talk to each other about how to advance each other's agendas. We acknowledge that they are separate; Timberland's job is to make boots and earn profit and City Year's mission is to put young people into service and transform American society. The [agendas are] separate and yet there are strategic ways that we can align the outcomes." Swartz has characterized this stage as "commercial," because it is analogous to a buyer-seller relationship dominated by the parties' search for specific value transactions.

The cornerstone for building a richer value exchange is the identification of overlapping missions and compatible values. Swartz, in the context of developing a new corporate strategy, had added the theme of "beliefs" to the company's prevailing themes of "boots" and "brand." This new dimension holds that the company and its employees should make a positive difference in society at large and that the corporate culture should foster involvement in confronting and solving problems within and outside the company. City Year holds a similar belief about affecting society, and its mission also promotes civic engagement, not just by its own youth corps members but also by corporations and other elements of society.

With the recognition of these commonalities, the magnitude and scope of the City Year–Timberland engagement broadened.

In 1991, Timberland became the financial sponsor of one of City Year's youth corps teams, first for a semester, then for a whole year.

In 1992, City Year organized a service day for Timberland employees, including Swartz. Devoted to renovating a New Hampshire adolescent treatment center, this hands-on experience was pivotal in cementing the relationship. It crystallized in Swartz's mind the value of direct community service by employees as a means of fostering team building, leadership development, interdepartmental relationships, project management abilities, and in general, a high-involvement culture wherein individual and collective efforts make a difference in outcomes within and outside the business. City Year made a presentation at the opening of a Timberland retail outlet and later to a Timberland international sales meeting. Swartz was elected to City Year's board of directors, and the company made a $1 million contribution, spread over three years. Timberland hired graduates from City Year's youth corps, and company employees participated in City Year's annual Serve-a-thon day.

In 1993, Timberland became the official supplier of the entire City Year uniform. This was important in terms of giving City Year a clearer identity in the public eye and publicizing that Timberland had an entire line of casual and outdoor apparel and was deeply committed to City Year.

In 1994, City Year expanded to a national presence, with 650 corps members in six cities. Timberland, as a founding national sponsor, made a five-year commitment totaling $5 million, and Swartz was named chair of the City Year board. Drawing on their expertise in group development, City Year staff led Timberland employees in team-building and diversity training, causing Swartz to observe: "Many companies pay thousands of dollars for this type of team-building skills. This is not philanthropy. I firmly believe that the minds we turn on here at Timberland explode our productivity and effectiveness." And Freitas has commented that "the role of employee is very similar to the role of citizen in City Year's construct. They urge you to take an interest and be active, to see that decisions are made well and that these decisions are not just someone else's problem. We try to build those behaviors and attitudes into Timberland." In this year, Timberland allotted its employees sixteen hours of paid time to engage in community service if they so chose, and they put in a total of 1,544 paid community service hours.

The City Year–Timberland relationship grew bigger, broader, and deeper during this transaction stage. Forms of value exchange multiplied, the resources deployed expanded greatly, and interactions intensified. The perceived mutual value of the alliance also grew. Benefit flow was two-way. Relative to a stage one (philanthropic) relationship, a stage two (transactional) relationship is a quantum leap in terms of importance to the partners. Chapter Five offers an analysis of the sources of value creation in this stage. The City Year–Timberland relationship, however, continued to evolve into the third stage on the Collaboration Continuum.

Integrative Stage

A relationship has arrived at the third, or integrative, stage when the partners' missions, people, and activities begin to experience more collective action and organizational integration. The relationship begins to look like a highly integrated joint venture that is central to both organizations' strategies. The magnitude and form of resource exchange increases, and joint activities broaden still further. Personnel interactions intensify, and in several of the third-stage relationships studied, one of the corporate partner's top executives had been named to the nonprofit partner's board of directors and had become engaged in the governance of that partner. Individual value creation escalates to joint value creation; each organization's culture is affected by the other's; processes and procedures are instituted to manage the growing complexity of the relationship. Ultimately, the alliance becomes institutionalized.

This third stage is the current *collaboration frontier* in cross-sector alliances. Relatively few NPOs and companies have advanced to this degree of integration, but those farsighted partners that have are reaping what they perceive to be significant benefits.

City Year and Timberland achieved higher levels of integration of their missions, organizations, and activities at this stage. Swartz described this "mutual mission relationship" as boundarylessness. "It's not them and us. It's just we are us and they are them and we are together us, too." Implicit in the introduction of this *we* is an ever-widening set of personal and organizational connections. The relationship network expands beyond the leaders and early proponents and converts. "Our organization and their organization, while not completely commingled, are much more linked," asserted Swartz. "It's not simply personal; it's also collective. While we remain separate organizations, when we come together to do things we become one organization." Swartz's acceptance of the chair of the City Year board represented a significant integration in the leadership function.

The alliance became more integrated into Timberland's core activities in 1995 when the company pilot-tested a new line of apparel called City Year Gear. Value statements like "Give Racism a Boot" and "Hike the Path to Justice" were associated with products such as backpacks and T-shirts that were marketed through Timberland's retail outlets with the profits going to benefit City Year. Although the products were well received by consumers and the salesforce, the project has not yet moved to a larger scale. Also in 1995, Timberland doubled the paid time employees could give to service to thirty-two hours.

In the integrative stage, partners' mutual commitment becomes sufficiently strong to withstand shocks. This was put to the test in 1995, when Timberland incurred losses for the first time since going public. Its stock price plummeted,[2] the resulting layoffs demoralized its employees, and both some insiders and some outsiders criticized Timberland's sizeable grants to City Year. At the same time, City Year was under stress because the newly elected, Republican-controlled Congress was proposing to eliminate the AmeriCorps program that provided 50 percent of City Year's national funding. This situation tested the value and the durability of the alliance, and Timberland did not renege on its commitment to City Year. Freitas explained: "I think that it is harder when business gets tough to justify any expense. But when business is good you should be asking the same questions. Nothing changes fundamentally. Why do you have this

$5 million program? It is easy to think that when business is great community enterprise is great. But if you buy the model that we are trying to create, you have to be able to say that this thing holds up under any business condition."

Swartz cited jointly collaborating to set up City Year operations in a major city as an example of the form that integrated action at this stage might take. He described how the successful launch of City Year corps teams in a new city was to become a performance goal for Timberland brand managers and how the City Year managers would help sales by enlisting Timberland retailers as City Year service partners. "We are working on a mission that while it supports our separate agendas, is really a mission focused and fashioned together, and that's a layer that I really want to continue to build."

In another example, Swartz drew a distinction between stage two and stage three behavior: Timberland's human resource vice president spent two days (twenty of her paid-time service hours) at City Year helping staff structure pay plans and labor policies. He saw this as stage two, or transactional, behavior. If the City Year–Timberland relationship had been in the stage three, or integrative, model when she gave this help, this time would have been seen as just part of her job, no different than time spent assisting one of Timberland's manufacturing plants. Instead of part of a transactional relationship, comparable to a commercial exchange, it would have been part of an equity-based relationship, comparable to a joint venture.

"[City Year and Timberland] share this vision of a new paradigm of how business and community relate and how you can do well by doing good," Alan Khazei stated. "We have really tried to push what Jeff calls the boundarylessness and are constantly inventing new ways of cooperation between the two organizations." Stage three organizational integration was manifested in Swartz's evolving role as chair of the City Year board. In his first tour as board chair Swartz felt "honored that they wanted me to serve." He explained that his attitude toward the role of board chair during his first term was, "It's their organization; you are a steward; you run cover for them; the board is a place where things get done that they want done." He considered his second term almost equivalent to a second full-time job in terms of practical hours spent. "I have acted," he continued, "like I'm at the helm of City Year. I'm holding management accountable to the standards. The board is forcing real change on these guys. I get to practice all those things that my company board tells me that I do wrong." Swartz used as his model the private investors who become the chairs of companies acquired through leveraged buyouts (LBOs): "In an LBO fund you have made your personal investment. Well, I've surely made mine at City Year. I'm going to treat it like that." Rather than a donation or a resource transfer, the funds and materials provided are considered to be like an equity investment in a partnership.

In 1997, Timberland increased employees' paid community service hours to forty per year, the most of any corporation. Timberland employees performed 7,536 paid community service hours in 1996, 17,455 in 1997, and 19,831 as of July 1998, which included about 12,000 hours from a companywide service day involving Timberland employees worldwide, an event planned and implemented jointly by City Year and Timberland staff.

CARE and Starbucks: Alliance Evolution

The collaboration between CARE and Starbucks offers an additional perspective on the evolution of alliance relationships. Formally launched in September 1991, the partnership was from the beginning more than one of traditional philanthropy. (Chapter Three examines how these partners connected in the first place.) Starbucks chairman and CEO Howard Schultz recalled promising Peter Blomquist, CARE's Northwest regional director, that "we would integrate CARE into every aspect of Starbucks' business."[3]

The principal initiating activity was the creation of a coffee sampler containing coffees from three countries in which CARE operated. Sold in Starbucks stores, with $2 from each sale going to

CARE, the sampler generated $62,000 for CARE in 1992. In this project Starbucks was using its business competencies and infrastructure to generate benefits to CARE. The partnership was also celebrated in January of that year at the opening of a new Starbucks store in Los Angeles. CARE in turn recognized Starbucks with its 1992 Northwest International Humanitarian Award. Through reciprocal public recognition of the partnership, the partners were positively reinforcing their alliance formation decision. Starbucks's corporate leaders also deepened their sense of engagement and commitment through experiential exposure, such as the visit Schultz and Starbucks senior vice president Dave Olsen made to a CARE water project in Guatemala.

In 1993, CARE bestowed upon Schultz its Corporate Leadership Award, and Starbucks increased its commitment with a $100,000 donation to a CARE land restoration project in Ethiopia, the birthplace of coffee. Starbucks also sponsored the first of a series of Kenny G concerts, the proceeds of which benefited CARE. The concert, sampler sales, and other donations generated an additional $103,000 for CARE in 1993.

These activities suggest a cause-related marketing relationship, and CARE had been thinking about the alliance that way, but Starbucks had not. Blomquist recalled using that term and being challenged by a Starbucks employee who said: "This is not a marketing partnership for us. That's not why we're doing it. To call it a cause-related marketing partnership implies a calculated business plan to advance a marketing agenda, and that doesn't resonate well with us. It started from a commitment to the values, and that's where it really lives inside here."

In fact the CARE relationship helped Starbucks elucidate its values. At the time the partnership was inaugurated, Olsen explained, "these values weren't even expressed on paper. The intent was expressed before the values were even really articulated except in conversations with Howard, Peter, and me. In what later became our mission statement one of our six guiding principles requires us to be basically good citizens of our communities, and that meant these communities in developing countries." Starbucks began to feature its partnership with CARE in its orientation for new hires. "Our relationship with CARE," Schultz observed, "has become a source of pride for our partners [Starbucks employees]."[4]

In 1994, Starbucks ratcheted up its commitment in magnitude and duration. It agreed to be a sponsor of CARE's fiftieth anniversary and made a funding commitment of $500,000, to be spread over three years. It also made CARE the center of its in-store and mail-order communication and promotion efforts in 1995. These larger resource flows were complemented by an increased people flow between the two organizations. As more Starbucks executives and staff became involved in CARE activities and some CARE staff spent time in Starbucks, the organizations' values and missions became more entwined, and joint learning and value creation increased. This is indicative of a relationship that is moving beyond traditional philanthropy to the transactional stage of two-way benefit flows and then to the stage of organizational integration, in which people from each organization became more deeply engaged in issues critical to the other.

In events epitomizing the integration on the people side, Blomquist was hired by Starbucks in 1997 to head up its newly formed company foundation, and Olsen was named to CARE's board in 1998. Commitment of both time and money had expanded significantly. By July 1998, Starbucks had become CARE's largest corporate donor; its cumulative direct contributions of $650,000, merchandise sales revenues of $481,000, and other donations of $112,000 added up to a grand total of $1.2 million.

Conversely, when Starbucks was criticized by Guatemalan labor activists for not helping coffee workers, it sought CARE's counsel and expertise to formulate a code of conduct for its coffee suppliers.

CARE's engagement in a process of creating its own global identity and Starbucks' engagement in global expansion now represent yet another opportunity for the partners jointly to generate new knowledge. Finally, the partnership constitutes a real-time alliance laboratory in which both organizations can learn how to effectively manage this and other such relationships.

The Nature Conservancy and Georgia-Pacific: Integration Progress and Challenges

The alliance between The Nature Conservancy (TNC) and Georgia-Pacific has progressed from the confrontational relationship described in Chapter One to the joint undertaking of a forest and resource management project that was primarily transactional but is beginning to enter the integrative stage.

Georgia-Pacific's relationship with conservation groups such as TNC, as Georgia-Pacific senior vice president John Rasor has summarized it, "has grown and matured over the years, from a one-shot public relations and tax opportunity into a long-term partnership. We're still in the business of growing and harvesting trees to supply raw materials to our paper and building products mills. However, in our environmental journey we have recognized that environmental stewardship is an important element in how we manage our mills and our nearly six million acres of commercial forest land. And cooperative partnerships and proactive alliances are a growing part of our environmental strategy and commitment to sustainability." (Chapter Four explores how TNC's and Georgia-Pacific's strategy changes fostered strategic fit.)

The first breakthrough in the basic relationship between TNC and Georgia-Pacific involved a North Carolina forest wetlands area known as the Lower Roanoke. Reflecting on the Roanoke agreement, TNC president John Sawhill remarked that it represented "an unprecedented level of cooperation between two traditional opponents . . . but times have changed. The Conservancy has recognized that in some ecosystems protecting rare plants and animals need not exclude economic activity, in this case, logging. Although seemingly counter to the prevailing environmental dogma, this represents an intriguing and cost-effective trend in conservation."

Now these two organizations' interactions have broadened, deepened, and intensified. Their missions are converging and their personnel are more involved at this incipient stage of organizational integration, as signaled by Georgia-Pacific CEO Pete Correll's membership on TNC's board of directors.

The benefits of an integrative relationship are attended by additional challenges. As the nature of The Nature Conservancy–Georgia-Pacific relationship has changed with its progression along the Collaboration Continuum, both organizations have had to relinquish increasing amounts of control, which has posed a threat to each along the way. When, for example, the two organizations were discussing whether to strategically collaborate in the joint management of the Lower Roanoke River forest lands, Georgia-Pacific's attorneys and accountants argued for a sale or donation to TNC rather than an ongoing and potentially restrictive joint land agreement. "There was concern at Georgia-Pacific about locking ourselves into something that would be bad for shareholders," explained senior communications manager Lynn Klein. "We might at some point want to sell the property." Though Georgia-Pacific has retained its right to sell the land at a later date, to minimize its loss of control, The Nature Conservancy has the right of first refusal if Georgia-Pacific decides to sell the land.

As the partnership has intensified and the once-separate reputations of the partners have become more closely aligned, each organization has also had to give up some degree of control over its image and brand. "We value most our reputation," observed Sawhill. "If we tarnish it in a partnership, we jeopardize our membership support and revenues." This partnership with a "big bad timber company" made TNC the subject of much controversy within the conservation community. One TNC executive noted that some environmental advocacy organizations saw TNC as a "free rider," coming in and making deals after the advocates had pressured the companies into action. Similarly, Georgia-Pacific's willingness to associate with "tree huggers" was questioned by other timber companies. As they chart a new path of partnership, both organizations face the challenge of overcoming long-standing stereotypes and prejudices within their respective communities.

Using the Continuum as a Framework

The foregoing examples clearly reveal that as cross-sector alliances pass through different stages, they evolve. The Collaboration Continuum can serve as a useful framework for thinking strategically about such changing alliances, both in assessing an existing collaboration and in planning its future. The framework can help managers answer three fundamental questions: Where are we? Where do we want to go? How do we get there? Figure 2.1 and Table 2.1 synthesize the framework and illustrate how it can help managers categorize the collaboration in which their organization is engaged and better understand how an alliance may change as it migrates from one stage to another.

Assessing a Changing Relationship

Figure 2.1 summarizes the collaborative relationship in each of the three stages: philanthropic, transactional, and integrative. As the relationship moves from stage to stage, the level of engagement of the two partners moves from low to high. The importance of the relationship to each collaborator's mission shifts from peripheral to strategic. The magnitude and nature of the resources allocated to the relationship expand significantly. The scope of activities encompassed by the partnership broadens. The partners' interactions intensify, and the managerial complexity of the alliance increases. Finally, the strategic value of the collaboration escalates from modest to major.

Figure 2.1 Collaboration Continuum.

	One	Two	Three
Relationship stage	Philanthropic	→ Transactional →	Integrative
Level of engagement	Low → → → → → → → → → → → → High		
Importance to mission	Peripheral → → → → → → → → → Strategic		
Magnitude of resources	Small → → → → → → → → → → → → Big		
Scope of activities	Narrow → → → → → → → → → → → Broad		
Interaction level	Infrequent → → → → → → → → → Intensive		
Managerial complexity	Simple → → → → → → → → → → Complex		
Strategic value	Modest → → → → → → → → → → → Major		

Understanding Continuum Dynamics

Decisions determine dynamics. Progression along the continuum is not automatic; it is the result of the partners' conscious acts and efforts. A relationship can, moreover, due to unintentional slippage or conscious decisions, regress to a previous stage.

Also, collaborative relationships can be located at any point on the continuum. The three stages are not single discrete locations; there are many points in between the stages. The characteristics ascribed to each stage appear in gradations as a multifaceted relationship evolves incrementally from one stage into another. Partners might for strategic or tactical reasons create an intentional hybrid, with some aspects of the collaboration being characteristic of one stage and others of a different stage. Partners who understand that the Collaboration Continuum is multifaceted can approach the development of their relationship in a sophisticated and systematic manner.

Thinking Strategically About an Evolving Collaboration

Table 2.1 summarizes the characteristics of partnerships in each of the three stages in terms of four key strategic dimensions, which are

Table 2.1. Collaboration Continuum: Partnership Characteristics.

	Philanthropic	Transactional	Integrative
Collaboration mind-set	Gratefulness and charity syndromes Minimal collaboration in defining activities Separateness	Partnering mind-set Increased understanding and trust	*We* mentality in place of *us versus them*
Strategic alignment	Minimal fit required beyond a shared interest in a particular issue area	Overlap in mission and values Shared visioning at top of organization	Broad scope of activities of strategic significance Relationship as strategic tool High mission mesh Shared values
Collaboration value	Generic resource transfer Unequal exchange of resources	Core competency exchange More equal exchange of resources Projects of limited scope and risk that demonstrate success	Projects identified and developed at all levels in the organization, with leadership support Joint benefit creation Need for value renewal Shared-equity investments for mutual "return"

Relationship management	Corporate contact person usually in community affairs or foundation; nonprofit contact person usually in development	Expanded personal relationships throughout the organizations	Expanded opportunities for direct employee involvement in relationship
	Corporate personnel have minimal personal connection to cause	Strong personal connection at leadership level	Deep personal relationships across organizations
	Project progress typically communicated via written status report	Emerging infrastructure, including relationship managers and communication channels	Culture of each organization influenced by the other
	Minimal performance expectations	Explicit performance expectations	Partner relationship managers
		Informal learning	Organizational integration in execution, including shared resources
			Incentive systems to encourage partnerships
			Active learning process

Note: Prepared with the assistance of Linda Carrigan.

analyzed in the subsequent four chapters. The first dimension, the *collaboration mind-set*, assesses the partners' fundamental approach to their relationship. Do the partners operate at arm's length or arm in arm? Is their relationship one of dependency or interdependency? Is their connection with the purpose passionate or perfunctory?

The second dimension is *strategic alignment*. How well does the collaboration fit the partners' missions, strategies, and values? Minimally? Is there overlap? Do they mesh? Can greater alignment be achieved so the partnership can move to the next stage?

The third dimension is *collaboration value*. Are the partners' resources being mobilized so as to generate as much value as possible? Are the partners leveraging their distinctive competencies and combining them synergistically so as to move to higher levels of value creation?

The fourth dimension is *relationship management*. Is the partnership a minimally managed collaboration? Is responsibility for the relationship an assigned duty? Are adequate incentives in place to foster collaboration? Are communication processes explicit? How high are performance expectations set, and how is accountability ensured?

Systematic thinking is essential to strategic planning, and the Collaboration Continuum is a useful reference for systematic analysis of a collaboration. Although integrative relationships have the highest strategic value on the continuum, other relationship stages perform important functions and may fit an organization's particular needs better at some times. This point is elaborated further in Chapter Six in discussing the collaboration portfolio approach to managing multiple relationships.

This continuum and strategic framework may also have more general applicability. Although the Collaboration Continuum is empirically derived from and focused on relationships between NPOs and corporations, preliminary research suggests that it might also be useful for categorizing and thinking strategically about relationships between NPOs and government entities or foundations.

Conclusion

To think strategically about cross-sector collaborations, you must have a framework that enables you to envision strategic options. The Collaboration Continuum is such a framework. It can help you categorize relationships and understand their defining characteristics as they evolve through the philanthropic, transactional, and integrative stages. Each stage exhibits important differences in engagement level, mission importance, resource deployment, scope of activities, interaction intensity, managerial complexity, and strategic value. Each stage is also characterized differently in terms of the key strategic dimensions of collaboration mind-set, strategic alignment, collaboration value, and relationship management. Where an alliance falls on the continuum is determined by the strategic choices and actions of its partners. Knowing where you are is critical to deciding where you want to be.

3

Making the Connection

As we saw in the last chapter, the Collaboration Continuum provides both for-profit and nonprofit managers with an important strategic tool for thinking systematically about the type of cross-sector alliance they have or wish to develop. Managers must hold this strategic perspective while also turning their attention to putting strategy into practice. The first practical problem in developing an alliance is locating the right organization with which to partner. The marketplace for cross-sector collaborations is fraught with imperfections and inefficiencies. Nonetheless, systematic searches are possible, and assistance from *market makers*, intermediary professional service organizations that help companies and nonprofits create alliances, is available. Once a potential partner has been located, then managers undertake the task of assessing its desirability, which means engaging in the getting acquainted process discussed later in this chapter. If the potential partner proves attractive, mutual bonding begins. As this chapter illustrates, this process can be facilitated by personally engaging top leaders with the cause and with their partners.

Searching

The *alliance marketplace*—the meeting ground and its accompanying mechanisms for organizations interested in cross-sector partnering—is currently underdeveloped and inefficient. Prospective partners lack good information sources about each other and easy ways to seek one another out. Information about individual nonprofits, in particular, can be hard to come by. Information is somewhat more readily available for corporations, for which public disclosure obligations are much more stringent. Nonprofits and corporations seeking to develop alliances that transcend the traditional charitable check-writing relationship particularly require factual information and experiential knowledge that are not widely available. The absence of a collaboration clearinghouse for matching interested parties hinders the expression of supply and demand forces. Yet alliances are springing up. The impediments to getting together are superable.

Making the connection is sometimes happenstance. Peter Benzing, a retired vice president of Bayer Corporation, recalled the beginning of that company's relationship with Bidwell Training Center: "Accidents happen. In November 1989, I sat next to a woman on an airplane, and we were talking about job creation. She said, 'Have you heard of the Bidwell Training Center?' and I said, 'Never heard of it.' So she arranged a visit, and I talked to [Bidwell founder, president, and CEO] Bill Strickland for a half an hour about his philosophy of job training." Benzing was immediately convinced that Bayer and Bidwell had important work to do together.

The CARE-Starbucks relationship, as recounted earlier, began with a cup of coffee. In 1989, when Peter Blomquist, director of CARE's Northwest regional office in Seattle, stopped in for a cup of coffee, Starbucks was just one of many local coffee shops. Reading the shop's brochure about where Starbucks sourced its coffee, Blomquist was struck by the overlap between the company's supply countries and the countries in which CARE operated. Although the serendipity factor may have been at work in bringing Starbucks to CARE's attention, the evolution that followed shows that actions rather than destiny produced the results. Recalled Blomquist: "There was a picture of the coffee buyer, Dave Olsen, and I figured that would be a good place to start. I got back to the office and called him." Beyond serendipity, this nonprofit manager was alert to leads; once he spotted an opportunity, he acted on it.

Systematic Search

In addition to becoming more consciously receptive to partnering and ready to spot potential partners, managers can engage in proactive search processes. A key identifier for a nonprofit manager to look for is a corporation's actual or potential connection with the NPO's specific social cause or target group. Managers can survey the abundant publications and information on corporations and on corporate giving and identify intersections of interest. On the presumption that companies engaged in one alliance are likely to be receptive to others, they can consult business and social sector publications for articles about ongoing cross-sector alliances. Businesspeople serving as NPO board members can often provide useful information about and access to potential corporate partners.

The task for a business manager searching the scarcer, less thorough, and more difficult to access information on nonprofits is facilitated when the company has a focused area of social sector engagement—for example, youth services, environment, or public education. If the projected involvement is geographically specific, in a particular city for instance, local funders or nonprofit associations might be able to narrow the list. A company's employees, because of their personal involvement in the community, are often excellent identifiers of potential partners. A company looking for nationwide collaboration would likely focus on the larger, well-known NPOs that operate throughout the country or seek a successful local nonprofit with high potential for scaling up to national operations.

For both for-profit and nonprofit managers, informal networks of personal and professional contacts often produce good leads, but these sources should supplement rather than substitute for systematic searches for candidates for partnering.

Market Makers

The process by which companies and NPOs find one another can often be facilitated by market makers. Public relations, advertising, and corporate communications firms have been particularly effective at extending their business and marketing expertise into the social sector, especially in cause-related marketing. It was Visa's advertising firm, Frankel, that came up with the idea of a cause-related campaign and conducted the consumer research that identified literacy as an appealing cause to credit card users. However, an executive from Karlitz & Company, an advertising firm that has helped establish cause-related marketing programs such as the one through which Lipton raises awareness and funds for the National Women's Cancer Research Alliance, has observed that "a lot of people are experimenting with cause-related marketing now because it is in. Those who are in it for the long run will stick it out while others may drop their programs. There may be an industry shake out." Companies and NPOs should thoroughly assess any cause-related marketing deal in terms of the relationship's strategic implications and organizational fit, and they should be wary of any market maker who aggressively pushes such a deal before it has been well assessed by the potential partners.

Community Wealth Ventures

A different approach to market making is illustrated by an organization that has recently begun drawing on its own partnering experience in the nonprofit sector to assist other organizations. Community Wealth Ventures was incorporated to provide advisory services on partnering. It is a for-profit subsidiary of the nonprofit Share-Our-Strength (SOS), an NPO founded in 1984 by Bill Shore to fight hunger.[1] SOS was a pioneer in fundraising through corporate partnerships, starting with its Taste of the Nation event. Leading chefs throughout the country donate their talents to this event, and ticket proceeds are distributed to antihunger organizations via SOS. This event has attracted corporate sponsors such as *Bon Appétit* magazine, MasterCard, and American Express and generated $4.4 million in 1997. American Express also partnered with SOS in the cause-related marketing campaign Charge Against Hunger, donating three cents to SOS for every dollar cardholders charged during the November and December holiday season. This campaign generated $21 million for SOS between 1993 and 1996 and also strengthened relationships between American Express and the participating restaurants, noticeably increasing card usage. By 1998, SOS had formed more than one hundred local and national partnerships with corporations, including Barnes and Noble, Evian, and Calphalon. Clearly, SOS had figured out how to make the alliance marketplace work for it, and this prompted it to teach what it had learned to others, as Bill Shore recalled: "For the first time nonprofit organizations were asking not how to get money from us but if they could get someone from SOS to train them how to do it themselves." Corporations, too, were seeking advice. "Six years ago," observed SOS development director Ashley Graham in 1998, "I was making corporate outreach calls all day long. Now they're calling us, and they're also asking us how we do what we do." Shore added: "It took a remarkably long time for it to click with me that SOS had an asset of our own which could be leveraged: our expertise. From then on it was just the technical question of how to structure building a formal capacity." Given the immaturity of the cross-sector alliance marketplace, there was no large body of extant knowledge about how to create such partnerships. Inasmuch as knowledge was being generated primarily by practice, SOS was able to capitalize on its experiential learning. The challenge was how to create for this marketable proprietary asset an organizational delivery system that would enable it to play a productive and remunerative role as an alliance market maker for NPOs and corporations.

To stimulate managers' creative thinking about new directions, CWV provides to its NPO clients a list of *community wealth opportunities*. These fall into two categories: community wealth partnerships—which include licensing arrangements, cause-related marketing programs, and joint ventures–and community wealth enterprises—NPO business ventures that provide products or services but do not necessarily involve a corporate partner. CWV then walks each client's staff and board members through a process that helps them identify the NPO's assets and brainstorm ideas for generating new revenue. "Nonprofits," Shore contends, "are worth a lot more than they think they are." Determining their true value is difficult because at present there are few transactions that can serve as reference points. Finding leveragable assets, a key task in CWV's methodology, is essential to strategic planning and value creation (and I return to this topic in Chapter Five). CWV also helps nonprofits establish partnerships and community wealth enterprises by assisting them with business and financial planning, legal structuring, and enterprise development, implementation, and evaluation.

The trend toward strategic philanthropy notwithstanding, Shore believes that most corporations are not yet fully practicing it. "One of the things that we're trying to do," he explained, "is to help companies think about how their philanthropy could be tied to their business outcomes. That is still a really radical idea to a lot of people. Some companies have such a wall between philanthropy and business that just getting people to start thinking about integration is 90 percent of it. The rest is just commonsense derivation." The CWV process helps companies understand the potential benefits of partnering with a nonprofit and choose the cause and the organization that best meet their business and social objectives.

Although CWV is a young organization, its services appear to be in strong demand, evidence of the growing strength of the alliance marketplace. These services respond to NPOs' and corporations' expressed needs for information and strategic guidance.

The Chicago Children's Choir

To further illustrate the alliance marketplace needs of nonprofits and the assistance that can be provided by market makers, we may turn to the experience of the Chicago Children's Choir, one of CWV's initial clients. The choir, dedicated to making a difference in young people's lives through musical excellence, was founded more than forty years ago by the First Unitarian Church. Then a small children's choir, it is today the largest choral music education program for youths in the United States, serving more than three thousand children from a variety of racial and cultural groups.

Chicago Children's Choir executive director Nancy Carstedt became interested in working with CWV after a meeting with Shore. "When I met Bill for the first time," she recalled, "I was struck by how closely community wealth creation met my thinking about a new direction for the children's choir." Annual choir tours abroad had always been difficult to fund, most of the choir members being from low-income, minority households that lacked the resources to pay for the trip. Carstedt believed the annual tour to be critical to the mission of the organization. Looking for ways to turn this cost center into a profit center, she thought "that a diverse group of young people traveling around the world and sharing their music could be a very powerful tool within a corporate partnership." Carstedt was intrigued by the idea of a community wealth enterprise as a means to supplement or even supplant the choir's traditional revenue sources.

According to Karen Aidem, CWV's first president, the children's choir faced an issue common to most nonprofits: "When you're running the treadmill every day," she observed, "you're trying to keep up with the next big donor and trying to figure out where the next $10,000 is coming from, you don't always have time to look five years out and ask, 'Are we sustainable?' and 'What do we do when this grant goes away.'" Carstedt was seeking answers to these questions when she first met Shore. She was able to hire CWV to help her identify opportunities for the choir thanks to a grant from the Chicago Community Trust. Many NPOs will need third-party payers if they choose to use the assistance of a firm like CWV, and foundations are the logical funding source as they have a strong interest in enabling their grantees to achieve financial sustainability.

In June 1998, in a day-long exercise, CWV took the board and staff of the Chicago Children's Choir through the process of understanding community wealth and identifying the NPO's leveragable assets and opportunities for community wealth-building programs. As a result, the choir has generated several leads for potential corporate partners and a list of ideas for community wealth enterprises, which include starting a choir school, marketing a curriculum, and selling a songbook. What CWV is providing seems analogous to the strategy formulation assistance consulting firms provide to corporations: an analytical framework and a systematic and interactive process to assess strengths and weaknesses and opportunities and threats.

"A lot of consultants," Carstedt observed, "come in and they leave you with some sort of document and that's it. But this has a much different feel to it. It has the feel of an ongoing relationship. As we venture into unknown territory it's critical to have that support." In particular, Carstedt acknowledged CWV's experience with partnership building to be a critical resource that the choir expects to continue to draw upon in forming and maintaining the partnerships that it hopes to develop. "We simply don't have the experience with that," she said. "We will need their help all the way through."

Carstedt's experience suggests that the role of the alliance market maker can usefully extend beyond the initial strategy consulting to partner identification, alliance negotiation, and collaboration management. It is important, however, that these services be aimed at empowering and enabling an organization to carry out the partnership itself. The creation of true strategic alliances cannot be contracted out.

Getting Acquainted

Having found each other, prospective partners need to get to know one another to ascertain whether they should connect. Such getting acquainted involves looking for personal chemistry as well as conducting due diligence on competency and character.

CARE and Starbucks

When CARE regional director Peter Blomquist cold called Starbucks's senior vice president of coffee, this number two executive answered his own phone. Recalled Dave Olsen, "While Peter was very intense, he was not pushy. We took each other seriously from the very beginning. I wasn't trying to be some greedy businessman, and he wasn't trying to be a pushy fundraiser. We began just by talking." Conversation, not elaborate proposals, is the currency of choice in this initial stage.

In addition to shared geographical interests, two other elements seemed to be important facilitators of the CARE-Starbucks connection. First, CARE's history and stature lent it institutional credibility. "I was immediately warmed," Olsen recalled, "by my own personal recollections of CARE packages. It had a meaning to me already. CARE had a reputation, maybe even more like a glow, that drew me toward it. So Peter came into a credibility that already existed in my own mind." Second, the personal interactions were positive, and as Blomquist commented, "As potential partners begin to get to know each other, the human chemistry piece is pretty important." He thought that his and Olsen's "style and interests worked well from the get-go."

Getting acquainted involves a willingness to invest time in an educational and assessment process. It is necessary to learn about a prospective partner's organization and assess the compatibility of that partner and the potential value of an alliance. Blomquist invited Olsen to participate in a CARE-sponsored seminar series on Indonesia, a Starbucks coffee source. The seminar brought together a wide range of academics, businesspeople, and others interested in the country. "That," Blomquist explained, "was a significant part of Dave's getting a broader and fuller feel for what CARE was, who some of CARE's connections and partners were in this community, and that advanced our discussions about a partnership." Olsen affirmed that the "seminar series served to validate in my mind CARE as a source of information, inspiration, and con-nections." Olsen gained further insight into CARE's work in 1991 when he visited a CARE literacy project in Kenya that reached two million school children, firsthand evidence of CARE's program deliv-ery competency. Blomquist arranged to have CARE country direc-tors and other personnel who came through the Seattle office meet Olsen, who was at the same time broadening Blomquist's interactions with other Starbucks managers. Blomquist also arranged for a meet-ing between CARE's then president, Phil Johnston, and Starbucks chairman and CEO Howard Schultz. This due diligence process incrementally broadened acquaintance networks and deepened the partners' understanding of one another's mission and competencies.

Olsen returned from Kenya, according to Schultz, "fired up and ready to formalize our involvement."[2] However, there were other non-profits seeking relationships with Starbucks at the time, and this caused management to reflect. Olsen recalled that the point of view was

> We better not fly off half-cocked here. We better think about this diligently and make sure we're making the right choice. I wouldn't say that we invested a huge amount of time in that process, although we did think about it. Every time we asked a question, CARE came back to the top of the list. Can they do the work? Are they involved in the right countries? Will they talk openly to us and listen intently to us? Do they have in their list of friends the kind of people we'd like to be associated with? On every level it looked to us like this was the right thing to do.

On CARE's side the corporate partner selection process rested primarily with Peter Blomquist as the Northwest regional director, as Starbucks was then a company local to that region. However, as the relationship neared consummation, he involved many of CARE's functionaries in the process, including CARE's president.

CARE's current due diligence process for potential corporate partners is illuminating. This nonprofit's culture, observed one manager, "is that everybody wants to be involved in every decision, so as soon as a fundraiser is talking to a company about a relationship, we let everybody know." A screening committee comprises representatives from every employee group. During the information-gathering phase anyone can send the committee comments or information about the candidate company. Committee members talk to the corporation about what the company wants to do, where it wants to do it, and what publicity and kind of relationship are sought. If a particular country is targeted for involvement by the company and the CARE director for that country objects, that will stop the partnership process. If the screening committee cannot reach consensus, the decision is passed up to the executive staff. A basic guiding principle is that "CARE seeks relationships with partners whose mission and values are compatible with what we are doing and with our core values."

CARE also uses this five-step framework to guide the corporate partner selection process:

1. *Verify* the facts. What we know; what we may know; what we don't know; what we may never know.
2. *Identify* stakeholders. Who cares about this decision, how much, and how large is their stake?
3. *Clarify* issues. Distinguish between legal, financial, management, and moral issues. Can you get the issues down to two sentences?
4. *Evaluate* options for action. There are always more options than the intuitive ones.
5. *Resolve* to take action. How do you know which option to take? Always take the option that is just and fair. Justice equals "walk in the shoes of all stakeholders." Fair equals "like situations get like treatment." If you can't decide, go back to step four.

It is also useful during the due diligence process to ascertain the perspectives of existing partners, commercial or social, on the candidate organization.

The Mind-Set Barrier

Often the getting acquainted process must overcome attitudes resistant to collaboration. For The Nature Conservancy (TNC) and Georgia-Pacific, old mind-sets and perceptions restricted, and continue to restrict, realization of their relationship's full potential. Some at Georgia-Pacific continue to associate TNC with "tree huggers," and some at TNC continue to view Georgia-Pacific as anticonservation. Rob Olszewski, Georgia-Pacific director of environmental affairs, said of the mind-set in the forest industry: "Some of the conservative foresters tend to group the environmental community together, rather than sorting through the vastly different organizations. There are still some cowboy foresters out there who feel like it's none of anybody's business what we do out there on the landscape."

As mentioned in Chapter Two, the Lower Roanoke River proposal, TNC's and Georgia-Pacific's first effort at joint land management, did not receive universal support. Georgia-Pacific's law and tax departments and some managers resisted the change. "Our law and tax people like to keep everything very clean," recalled senior communications manager Lynn Klein. "They said, 'Why don't you just sell it to them or donate it, and that way it's clean and we're out of there.'" Senior vice president John Rasor looked to Klein to build the case for this new kind of agreement. "We ended up not yielding to the tax people," Klein recalled, "and the long-term benefits have been good. It has probably made people a little bit more willing and open to look at new relationships."

TNC president John Sawhill commented that "the biggest difficulty" in overcoming traditional ways of doing business "was a mind-set on both sides that was grooved in the traditional way of doing business. We wanted to buy their land—that's the way we'd always operated. And they said let's think about a different way of accomplishing your objectives, because we're not going to sell this to you. Abandoning some of our traditional ways of thinking enabled us to move forward."

It is also important to recognize that resistance to cross-sector partnering may reflect genuine differences in values and perceived missions rather than irrational stereotyping and aversion to change. Sorting out the true causes of resistance is an important task in this phase of making the connection.

Engaging Top Leadership

Every successful strategic alliance studied had significant support and direct involvement from top leaders in the partnering organizations. Absence of this leadership engagement is evidence that a relationship has not reached the level of strategic importance.

Top managers are alliance authorizers. The go-ahead decision for the Starbucks alliance with CARE was made at the top. Recalled Starbucks' Howard Schultz, "Dave [Olsen] talked to me about CARE and we both liked its approach. We liked the idea of giving back to coffee-origin countries. But at that point we were not in a position to give. We were still losing money—more than $1 million in that year alone. But Dave and I set a goal: once the company became profitable, we would start donating to CARE."[3] Central to this decision were the principals' personal and corporate values. As Olsen commented, "On a very personal level, I knew that this was something that I wanted to be associated with, business not just for its own sake in the old, the-business-of-America-is-business sense, but business as a well-balanced instrument of positive impact in the world. I was looking for opportunities to explore and express that. I felt the same feeling from Howard Schultz, and at that time there were very few other senior people in the company, so the two of us could pretty much do anything we wanted."

Similarly, a manager of The College Fund (UNCF) remarked about its relationship with Merck: "For our partnerships we mandate top echelon support, because when you need to change the direction of the ship, you need the captain at the helm. You can't change the direction by committee. Merck's CEO is genuinely committed to this whole process. He really believes in what he's doing. There is also senior-level involvement from our end. Our president took the leadership in setting this partnership up."

An executive with Beginning with Children, a nonprofit that runs a public school in New York in partnership with Pfizer, a pharmaceutical company, observed that when Beginning with Children opens "a new school, the Pfizer CEO will be there. Yet, I know that is not always the case with other partnerships." An MCI WorldCom manager emphasized that this expectation also holds for the nonprofit: "We don't sign partnerships unless they're brought all the way up to the highest-ranking level of the nonprofits. We want to be a strategic partner with these nonprofits; we don't want to be just one of fifty partners."

Reflecting on the Time Warner alliance with the literacy promoter Time to Read, a company executive stressed that top support breeds organizational acceptance: "If our CEO didn't feel really, really strongly about that, none of this would happen. That has to be the driver. He cares about it, and the support staff cares about it, and we connect the dots from the top to the bottom. That's why this is a fully functional, fully integrated, highly effective program. One of our competitors has a bunch of magazines, too, but its culture doesn't support this kind of work." The original partners in this alliance were Time, Inc., and Time to Read, and a sign that the corporate support had been well institutionalized was the alliance's uninterrupted continuation when Time merged with Warner.

With a project champion, a new undertaking will likely thrive; without one, it may well fade. That not all of Bayer and the Bidwell Training Center's attempts to collaborate have had staying power is a consequence of project sponsors' having left. Bayer executives are the first to admit that a Bidwell project with the AGFA division of Bayer has not lived up to expectations. Observed Bayer's

Benzing: "That connection hasn't done all that well. We need to rejuvenate it. The people who were enthusiastic and a part of it left the company. There are some thoughts to get that back. We need to get it back. We need to get some AGFA people to visit Bidwell. The method is to bring people [into Bidwell] and have them convince themselves." A similar fate struck a ceramics project with the departure of that division's president. Without a champion to see it through, the project has yet to get off the ground, in spite of the alliance's great success in other projects.

Creating Personal Connections and Relationships

Because top management engagement is critical to partnership success, it is important for managers to know how it is brought about. My research reveals that in cross-sector social purpose collaborations, unlike commercial business alliances, an essential ingredient for strong leadership involvement is an emotional connection. Institutional partnerships are created, nurtured, and extended by people. Social purpose partnerships appear to be motivationally fueled by the emotional connection individuals make with the social mission and with their counterparts in the other organization. The mission connection is the driver, and the personal relationships are the glue that binds the organizations together.

Timberland's Jeff Swartz insists that alliance building is "deeply, deeply personal stuff. The key to this is finding a relationship that can profoundly and personally work. The best relationships that Timberland has are deeply personal relationships, whether with customers or suppliers or with City Year. There is no question about the importance of my connection to Alan Khazei and of five Timberland managers with five City Year managers."

Of the Perinis' personal connection with the Jimmy Fund, a family member remarked: "My great-grandfather, grandfather, and brother all died from cancer. Because of it I just feel more passionate about raising money for the Jimmy Fund. My mom and dad have been unbelievable in supporting the Fund. My mom was always the number one fundraiser for the Jimmy Walk, raising like $30,000." As a spokesperson for the Jimmy Fund pointed out, "Everyone has been touched by cancer in some way. It knows no social status." The relationship between the Perini Corporation and the Jimmy Fund is the oldest alliance in this study, and its staying power is impressive. But such personal connections are subject to generational dilution. "As time goes on, and if my dad leaves the company," the family member continued, "I don't think that there are too many younger employees who feel that much of a connection to the Jimmy Fund."

For alliances to be sustainable there must be strong commitment and good chemistry at the top level. Observed Starbucks's Olsen, "This partnership has changed my life and Peter Blomquist's life." For these two protagonists the partnership has been a profoundly personal passion. But the connections across the organizations are broader than just the connections between two individuals. Starbucks hosted a party to honor retiring CARE president Phil Johnston in 1996 and has developed a close relationship with his successor, Peter Bell. Olsen has developed strong relationships with CARE country managers, particularly in Guatemala.

Personal relationships throughout The Nature Conservancy–Georgia-Pacific collaboration drove and continue to drive the alliance. These relationships are requisite to building mutual trust. CEOs Pete Correll and John Sawhill became acquainted while serving on the President's Council for Sustainable Development. Sawhill asked Correll to serve on TNC's board starting in September 1995, and the two traveled together to Belize to examine a TNC project. As their professional and personal relationship grows through direct interaction, so too does the depth of the organizational relationship.

The relationship between Sawhill and Correll sends a strong message to their respective organizations about the importance of the collaboration and gives employees the liberty to actively engage in the partnership. Georgia-Pacific's Rob Olszewski commented on the impact of this key relationship at Georgia-Pacific: "Pete and John have a pretty good relationship personally and everybody knows that. If Pete feels like it's OK to deal with these people—he's interested in them, he's on their board, and he's gone on trips with Sawhill—then that conveys that it's OK to work with these folks too. I think that gives a signal from the top that nobody is going to criticize you if you're caught off with The Nature Conservancy folks somewhere one day."

Bill Strickland and Peter Benzing have been driving forces in developing the relationship between Bidwell and Bayer. Recognizing the need to engage Bayer's senior leadership, Benzing invited then president of Bayer Corporation Konrad Weis to visit Bidwell. Recalled Benzing: "I knew he was interested in different approaches, and he caught on immediately too. He saw the same things that I and the other business leaders had seen and became a strong supporter." The relationship between the organizations subsequently broadened as Weis introduced personnel from other Bayer divisions, such as agriculture, to Bidwell. Nor can Strickland's impact on the partnership be overestimated. "Bill is a person of vision," emphasized Bayer Foundation executive director Sande Deitch. "He not only has vision, but he also has the energy to make things happen. He could have left many times, but did not because he knew he had a job to do here. I've always admired that as well. Through his personal example he motivates a lot of people and certainly has motivated me."

"The whole story is the story of people working with their friends," Benzing emphasized. Deitch concurred: "It's about people and making things happen, definitely. It's not always about cash. Money doesn't do any work and doesn't have any ideas. You have to have people." The partnership's staying power derives from the personal relationships that have developed because of individuals' personal interest in and connection to Bidwell. "The method is to bring people in here and have them convince themselves," explained Strickland. Visitors to Bidwell eat a gourmet lunch prepared by students in the culinary program, observe students in a travel agent program learning in real time on a computerized reservation system, view the pharmacy tech training program's pharmacy, see the state-of-the-art auditorium and recording equipment, and feel the spirit. "Once you see this facility and meet the people here, it's infectious," remarked a Bayer executive. "You just want to be involved. And we're a little bit selfish, in that we get something out of it too. Enlightened self-interest, we call it."

There are numerous examples of visitors turned converts. Sony executive Scott Bartlett did not know Bidwell personally when he came to visit because Sony was considering a collaboration. He left it a friend, remarking: "This is a pretty interesting place. I'll be back." Companies enter relationships with NPOs because of the substance and spirit of a program; the relationships are sustained because of the friendships formed.

Motivating through direct service exposure or engagement is often highly effective in creating a connection. The service day City Year organized for Timberland employees and top management provided an opportunity for Timberland COO Swartz to witness the positive and powerful team-building and motivational effects of community service and the City Year alliance. This proved to be a critical juncture in the relationship between the organizations.

The depth and strength of a relationship increases as the partners' employees engage in direct volunteer service. A Time Warner manager describing the involvement of the employee tutors in the Time to Read program remarked, "The participants and the employees were gathered for an introduction period, and I don't know who was more excited, the kids or the tutors. Everybody loves it. The brightest young journalists are involved with these kids in a way that is really, really life changing." A representative of the Off the Street Club, one of the community nonprofits collaborating in Time to Read, recounted this anecdote about the impact of the program:

A young man got in this program when he was a little boy. It was his first experience ever outside of his neighborhood. His first experience ever with people of other races. And you wonder, over the years, what kind of effect it has? Well, about ten years later when he was a grown man and traveling with my family, our plane stopped in Minneapolis. He went to the telephone and I thought, "What the heck? How could he know somebody here?" Out of his wallet, this grown man took a tattered piece of paper. It was the phone number of the first tutor he had in the Time to Read program. The lady had moved to Minneapolis. He carried it in his wallet for ten years because she meant so much to him. She was the first human being who gave him a sense of self. To me it was the ultimate endorsement of people who mentor and give up their time and of companies like Time Warner who really spend money on this stuff. It's changing people.

Conclusion

Strategic alliances are formed when partners make powerful connections with one other. The first complication is finding prospective partners. Discovery in the immature, underdeveloped, and imperfect alliance marketplace is hindered by information deficiencies. Until the cyberspace information explosion remedies this, partner matching might seem happenstance. But although serendipitous encounters play a role, being on the lookout for and predisposed to work with potential partners is what converts opportunities into action. Systematic searches are feasible using published information on organizations' partnering activities and areas of interest and drawing on the advice and contacts of board members, employees, colleagues, and grantmakers. Market makers, intermediary service organizations, can facilitate the matching process by helping potential partners identify their leveragable assets, locate suitable candidate collaborators, and formulate cooperation agreements.

Identifying capabilities and resources that might be useful to another organization, the magnets that might attract potential partners, is an important step. Assessing internal weaknesses reveals the compensating strengths to search for in possible allies. Having found one another, potential partners must get acquainted and assess their mutual compatibilities and competencies. It is important that top leadership, being the authorizers, legitimizers, and motivators for successful alliances, be engaged in this initial exploratory process. Such engagement tends to be motivated by an emotional connection with the social purpose and by strong interpersonal relationships. Passion for a cause can tap energy throughout an organization. Witnessing and experiencing a social service and interacting with program beneficiaries can create connection and be a powerful force for propelling an alliance forward. The deeper and broader the connections with purpose and people, the more solid the alliance's foundations.

4

Ensuring Strategic Fit

Once you have found a potential partner and have begun to get connected with this organization and its people, finding the right fit becomes the critical task for culminating the connection. The more central an alliance's purpose to the partners' missions, strategies, and values, the more important and vigorous the relationship is likely to be. Finding the right fit is a process that entails an investment of time and commitment to dialogue. The alignment task involves meshing missions, matching needs and capabilities, and overlapping values. Full fit may not be instantaneous but rather discovered as the partners experiment and grow together. Shared visioning sustains present and enriches future fit. Strategic fit also means fitting with the external environment, so this chapter ends with an examination of the strategy of obsolescence and reformulation that can lead to new collaboration.

Clarifying Purpose and Fit

"It's really important," The Nature Conservancy's John Sawhill advised, "to narrow down exactly what you're both trying to accomplish, where your interests overlap, and who bears what costs. You've got to be very, very explicit up front on both sides about what you really want out of the relationship."

A Reebok executive stressed how critically important and primary the fitting task is: "You can't overestimate the importance of finding the right fit with your partners. That investment is 85 percent of the work. You can't just say, 'They're well known, let's do it with them.' You have to say, 'We have customers and they have members; do these look like the same people?' If they do, you're more likely to win."

"We talked about fit and values up front," observed a Visa manager. "We were each very forthright in the beginning." A manager at Visa's NPO partner, Reading Is Fundamental, counseled, "The basic question in any of these marketing relationships is, 'What does this marketing campaign do to promote the mission of the organization?' If you don't have a good answer to that, you shouldn't be in the relationship." A Merck spokesperson commented, "Partnerships are hard to come by. A lot of work up-front has to be done before you can have a partnership. You are trying to meld goals and activities. It makes the research up-front to find out whether or not this is the right kind of partnership very important."

Developing a *partnership purpose and fit statement* is a useful initial joint exercise. Prospective partners should answer the following questions.

- What are you trying to accomplish through the collaboration?

- Where does your mission overlap with the potential partner's mission?

- Do you and your potential partner share an interest in a common group of people?

- Do your needs match up with your partner's capabilities, and vice versa?

- Would the collaboration contribute significantly to your overall strategy?

- Are your values compatible with your prospective partner's?

The answers form the organization's partnership purpose and fit statement. Each organization should answer these questions separately, in order to clarify precisely what it is trying to accomplish through the alliance and how it perceives the goodness of fit with the prospective partner. The organizations should then compare their respective answers to ascertain their degree of congruence and compatibility. This becomes a starting point for jointly clarifying purpose and adjusting the alliance's design to ensure strategic alignment—although the exercise might also lead to the conclusion that the organizations' purposes are incompatible or that acceptable fit is unattainable.

Organizations that are currently participating in alliances and that cannot state clearly the purpose and strategic fit for *both* partners should go through the process of formulating a partnership purpose and fit statement. If purpose and fit are clear and consistent across the partners, they should be written down in order to make this expressed common understanding accessible to others in the organizations.

The remainder of this chapter examines the nature of strategic alignment and the process of achieving it.

Aligning Mission, Strategy, and Values

Managers must consider whether organizational missions mesh, whether the alliance is equally important to both partners, whether partners' various needs and capabilities can be integrated, and whether the partners have enough organizational values in common.

Mission Mesh

Sometimes fit between missions is direct, as was the case with CARE and Starbucks's shared concern about the well-being of the people in coffee-growing countries. Similarly, a Time Warner manager noted that that company readily matched up with the nonprofit literacy promoter Time to Read: "We're focused on literacy.

We have good resources. The employees care about it. The senior management cares about it. It's just an obvious and excellent fit for us. We support the field of literacy in every sensible way." The executive added, however, that "there was a lot of research done at the beginning to find an area that was underserved; it's not like because we had these magazines [that could be used as reading materials] we decided to give them away." Ralston Purina's business interest in increasing the pet population coincided with the American Humane Association's social concern about reducing animal euthanasia. Pfizer's logical concern about the conditions in the economically depressed Brooklyn neighborhood surrounding its original production facilities fit well with Beginning with Children's development of a local school there.

In other instances fit may not be so obvious, yet deeper exploration will uncover alignments. Visa's credit card business had no direct interest in literacy promotion, yet the consumer research that revealed Visa cardholders' interest in this cause created relevancy and the basis for a partnership with Reading Is Fundamental. Similarly, although it had no focused cause that would tie directly into Nordstrom's retailing business, the Seattle United Way's support of multiple groups throughout the community fit well with Nordstrom's values and market. Believing that support of a single specific cause might unfairly impose on employees' individual beliefs and preferences, Nordstrom found United Way's broad range of supported services appealing. Moreover, United Way's extensive geographical reach earned Nordstrom goodwill in each of the communities in which it had stores.

Strategic Centrality

The more central the alliance is to each partner's mission and strategy, the stronger will be the partnership. The alliance between City Year and Timberland is particularly illuminating in terms of the challenges and payoffs of achieving strategic centrality. Once they began communicating and interacting, City Year and Timberland productively identified points where their missions coincided, and they developed a positive path toward future collaboration benefits. But this did not happen automatically. Timberland vice president Ken Freitas remarked, "There are difficulties in bringing together two organizations that in many respects have such rich common ground, because in other respects they are run and operated very differently. You have to push against the natural forces that pull you apart." To counter the centrifugal pressures generated by the organizations' different worlds, countervailing centripetal forces must be developed around a shared mission and vision to draw the two organizations together.

Timberland COO Jeff Swartz pointed to a failed partnership with a major environmental organization that illustrated the difficulty of this task. "That organization was not prepared to and did not want to take a mutual mission perspective," he explained. "They wanted stuff from us, period. We never ever got to the place where we could talk about what was good for each organization." Freitas elaborated: "The philosophy of that nonprofit was not related to Timberland's philosophy of full engagement of every individual to make this [partnership] happen today. Their philosophy was to work through existing defined channels and [to say] only this kind of activity is relevant. So that got to be somewhat limiting, and you can't have the depth of commitment, so we ended it."

In contrast, Timberland's relationship with City Year has become central to both organizations' core strategies. "The collaboration is integral to [City Year's] overall strategy," explained cofounder Alan Khazei. "Our whole core theory is about citizenship, so it's really essential to our mission that we try and involve business in what we are doing." Much the same is true for Timberland, according to Swartz: "Community service is one of our five business strategies, and the transformative relationship with City Year is central to that. It's an explicit business strategy and it's part of everything we do; it's part of every presentation we make to financial analysts."

Freitas emphasized the relevance of the alliance to Timberland's underlying philosophies: "We have to have a clear and powerful identity as a group of people, and that identity has to be a source of our success. This requires a strong commitment from employees. It needs to be much different than the typical exchange of value. One of our philosophies is that there's room for the whole person at Timberland. In fact, we kind of demand the whole person here; we want you to be an engaged, active participant. And the City Year relationship has been a tangible example of that philosophy put into practice." Moreover, the City Year relationship provided "good evidence" to consumers that Timberland was serious as it pitched the importance of community involvement and the company's association with such involvement. Similarly, cofounder Michael Brown affirmed that for City Year, "Timberland became a symbol within the organization of this whole concept of civic engagement and the role the private sector can play in social change."

Strategic centrality created an overlapping of purpose that motivated both organizations to invest heavily in the relationship. Because the collaboration was seen as integral to its mission and strategy, Timberland did not cut back on its financial commitment even when the company incurred sizeable losses in 1995. Over time the interaction even influenced both organizations' continued development and elaboration of their respective philosophies in the intersecting dimension of their missions. Because it was perceived as increasingly central to organizational strategies, the relationship elicited continuing top-level attention. Thus the alliance both fed the strategic fit and fed on it.

Matching Needs and Capabilities

Sometimes fit centers around specific operating needs and the capabilities required to meet them. Bayer Corporation vice president Peter Benzing's intimate familiarity with Bayer's hiring patterns and the challenges of finding well-trained lab technicians had immediately convinced him that Bayer and Pittsburgh's Bidwell Training Center had high collaboration potential. Pittsburgh's industrial base had undergone substantial change with which the labor force had not kept pace. In Bidwell's proven record of providing customized job training to inner-city individuals to prepare them to work at various companies in the Pittsburgh area, Benzing believed he had discovered a solution to Bayer's hiring challenges for its Pittsburgh plant. He saw in entry-level lab technician training a direct route to hiring some of the most able dislocated and disadvantaged workers. Bidwell, in turn, had a continuing need to find job placement opportunities for its inner-city target group, for which it would tailor training specifically to available opportunities. There was clearly congruency of needs and capabilities between the company and the nonprofit.

"You need to be invested in something that has to do with your business," emphasized a Bayer executive. "With a partnership like this, you need to have a two-way street. You need to be able to give and to get. For example, we're a science-based company. It makes business sense for us to support science education. Sometimes businesses get involved in things that are so far-fetched that they're mainly public relations programs. Now, it's not that we don't get good public relations from being involved, but we have a core reason to be involved."

Added executive director of the Bayer Foundation, Sande Deitch: "I always say that Bayer's not in the business to give money away. We're in the business to make money. So when you have a relationship that is supportive of our business goals, which this is, it's a natural."

Likewise, Merck's and Hewlett-Packard's businesses are intimately and ultimately linked to the supply of trained scientists and this made engagement with a nonprofit for the purpose of strengthening science education a clear fit for each company, as outlined in Chapter One. A Merck manager flagged an additional partner selection criterion: "[Partners] must have the ability, dedication, and structure to be able to implement the program that both partners agree to." Although managers examine these capabilities at a general level in the due diligence process described in the previous chapter, managers must revisit them once the purpose and parameters of a specific partnership have been delineated.

Overlapping Values

Compatibility of institutional values is integral to sustainable collaboration. Partners need not have completely congruent values, but the differences need to be within acceptable limits. Certain conflicting values will be collaboration stoppers. City Year's involvement with youths, for example, has led it to proscribe partnering with corporations in the liquor and tobacco industries.

That values as well as needs reinforce a relationship is evidenced by Bidwell's alliance with Bayer. Unlike many nonprofits, Bidwell Training Center shares Bayer's market orientation. "The fundamental thing that attracted me to the outfit," recalled Benzing, "was that it was completely market oriented. It didn't do any training if there were no jobs. The objective is to get people jobs and if there is no job there is no point in training people. In fact, Bill [Strickland] had a history and has demonstrated that when a training program has run out of a market he will stop the program for a year, two years, whatever, and then start it again when the market comes back. That appealed to my corporate sense of market orientation."

Bidwell has been successful in building partnerships with a number of corporations because Strickland understands how to find a market and "make himself relevant." A similar values congruency between Pfizer and Beginning with Children is no doubt in part a function of both having private sector mentalities, because the founders of this NPO migrated from the business sector.

Sometimes, as at Timberland, the birth of an alliance triggers a connection that becomes a cornerstone of a company's values. It was the alliance with City Year that fostered Swartz's integration of beliefs and community service into the center of the Timberland's strategy and culture. Reebok's partnering with Amnesty International, starting with support for a world music tour, also brought out a company value. As one Reebok executive explained: "The connection that [Reebok] CEO Paul Fireman saw was between athletic shoes and clothing being about freedom and making a personal statement about wearing what you want to wear and being who you want to be. And he saw a connection to young people, and this tour was about young people and a certain spirit. There was a lot of personal, high-level attraction to this cause." Not only did Reebok's $10 million investment in the tour exceed that year's advertising budget but it led the corporation to embrace human rights as a core value and continue its partnership with Amnesty International over ten years.

But this Reebok executive also noted that taking a strong, value-based stance brings challenges: "The harder you work at a cause, the harder it gets. You're always being tested on your commitment, and that's not necessarily a bad thing if it turns out right. I don't think cause-related marketing has that same onus placed on it. If you've made the issue part of your corporate charter, then you're going to get into all the hard stuff. If you've made it part of your Spring '99 campaign, you probably won't run into those issues."

Starbucks's commitment to assist coffee-growing communities encountered similar challenges and tests of commitment from labor activists.

Growing Together

Strategic alliances should grow over time, producing a deeper fit, more evolved objectives, and improved abilities on both sides.

Small Beginnings and Bolder Ventures

Sometimes strategic fit involves a discovery process—the partners explore a limited collaborative activity as a means to get to know one another better and test their compatibility. Recall that City Year's relationship with Timberland began with some free boots and a service project, and Starbucks's involvement with CARE with participation in a seminar. Serious relationships, organizational and interpersonal, should not be rushed.

As a relationship evolves, new needs and new areas of cooperation can emerge. For example, the strategic significance of its relationship with CARE became more important to Starbucks over time. Explained Starbucks senior vice president Dave Olsen: "While values drove the bulk of this [partnership], something else began to emerge. As we started gaining presence as a brand, we needed to make sure that we were delivering on our comprehensive promise to our customers, not just a good cup of coffee and good service. Our concern was also fueled by growing awareness of the situation faced primarily by apparel and footwear companies regarding working conditions and human rights in developing countries. We realized that we had to manage this as an issue as well as an expression of our core values."

And chairman and CEO Howard Schultz remarked, "Precisely because of our CARE donations, activists groups knew we were concerned about issues impacting Third World coffee growing companies. . . . The downside of being responsible and responsive is that it makes you vulnerable to an ever-wider array of special interest groups and individuals with diverse and sometimes unclear agendas."[1] When Starbucks turned to CARE for advice on how to handle these issues, the organizations entered a new dimension of collaboration.

Similarly, the success of the Lower Roanoke River project prompted The Nature Conservancy (TNC) and Georgia-Pacific to explore additional partnership opportunities. Each of Georgia-Pacific's key resource offices is now responsible for developing a plan around the company's new eleven-point Forest Resources Environmental Strategy, which includes actively seeking out cooperative partners and recognizing special sites. Thus, within an overall framework and guiding principles promulgated by the corporate office, individual profit centers or resource offices develop and implement environmental initiatives and partnerships appropriate to their local areas. Georgia-Pacific and TNC are currently working together on projects in a number of states.

As partnerships evolve they build internal focus and capability for partnering and, perhaps more important, mutual trust. Each cooperative activity brings a deeper understanding and appreciation of one another's capabilities and resources and an expanded perspective on future possibilities for the collaboration. Without this foundation, organizations would be unable to attain long-term success with higher-risk projects. In terms of the Collaboration Continuum, the Roanoke project was a transactional stage alliance to which specific distinctive resources were contributed but which required joint management and significant involvement at multiple operating levels for its implementation, which moved it toward greater organizational integration.

As Georgia-Pacific and TNC have developed their partnership, they have struggled to maintain a balance between maximizing the value of the mutual benefit flow and minimizing potential risks. In the early stages of the relationship, TNC was most interested in the traditional land sale or donation, a one-way value transfer from Georgia-Pacific to TNC that minimized risk for both. As the relationship has evolved, the stakes have increased. The Lower Roanoke River deal clearly set a precedent for a new kind of partnership, yet the land itself was not a high-priority, high-producing site for Georgia-Pacific. The company did not stand to lose much if the partnership failed. A follow-on project in the Altamaha River area of south Georgia, because the area contains highly productive timber lands, was a greater challenge than Roanoke. Georgia-Pacific has more at stake in this deal. But had it not been for the demonstrated success and value creation of the Roanoke project, the partnership could not have even considered the Altamaha River project. "You walk before you run," explained Georgia-Pacific's director of environmental affairs Rob Olszewski. "You don't want to get your extremely valuable assets too committed before you know your partner and how they think. These are all steps of an evolving relationship."

The Collaboration Multiplier

Collaboration breeds more collaboration. Partnering effectively affords companies and NPOs the skills and confidence to undertake other collaborations, not only with one another but also with new partners. This learning dividend from partnering creates a social capital multiplier effect as more organizations and individuals are brought into collaborative undertakings. Each additional alliance and set of relationships represent societal assets that further social purpose cooperation.

The success of their own collaboration, for example, disposed TNC and Georgia-Pacific to be receptive to innovative agreements with other organizations. "Our experience with the Lower Roanoke project," remarked Georgia-Pacific senior vice president John Rasor, "has spawned other innovative conservation agreements. In Florida, our foresters sold the development rights to more than thirty thousand acres to the state of Florida. Abiding by mutually agreeable forest management plans, we still manage our lands for timber production, but the state gets an assurance against commercial development of those properties. They were able to accomplish this without taking our lands off the tax roles and without assuming management costs."

Similarly, the success of Bidwell's chemical technician training program sparked interest from the statehouse to corporate boardrooms, leading Bidwell to mobilize government entities, other corporations, and educational institutions. Bidwell CEO Bill Strickland relates the story of engaging state government leadership:

> Bill Lieberman, an established Pittsburgh Republican leader and businessman, knew the majority leader of the Pennsylvania House of Representatives. The leader is a white Republican from a white working-class neigh-

borhood in the eastern part of the state, who might not have been expected to be sympathetic to an African American–led institution in Western Pennsylvania. Mr. Lieberman brought the majority leader to Bidwell, and I gave him the same tour as anybody else. At the end of the tour he said, "This is a hell of a program. This is extraordinary." I said, "Well, the problem, Mr. Leader, is I can't find any money to run it, as strange as that may sound. I have outstripped my funding. Government programs are not designed to do what you see going on here. And I'm down to my last nickel." He says, "Well, we'll see about that." And the long and short of it is that he has embraced this program and gotten the Appropriations Committee to embrace this program. Now they've got their model training program and we got an appropriation directly from the state, the only job training center in Pennsylvania where that happened. They want us to consider replicating the model. That's the quid pro quo. And the Appropriations Committee had their hearings at Bidwell. That's the first time in the history of the state that that's ever happened.

A successful collaboration effectively enticed government into supporting replication of the alliance model. Bidwell's advisory committee subsequently identified additional training needs facing Pittsburgh-area corporations. The end of the millennium found Bidwell and Bayer building support among area corporations for two new programs—for chemical process technicians and for polymer technicians, both highly specialized, highly skilled jobs for which few schools offer training. To deliver the hands-on training that Bidwell has proved to be so successful, these two programs will require further capital investment—approximately a million dollars in equipment and another million or two for the building. Such resource requirements called for another collaboration coalition.

Bidwell collaborated with other academic institutions to develop these programs. Again, a network connection facilitated a key contact. A recent supporter of Bidwell's lab technician program, a BASF Corporation plant in the Pittsburgh area, also operates a large plant in Freeport, Texas, where, jointly with Dow Chemical Corporation and the Brazosport Community College of Lake Jackson, Texas, it runs a highly successful training program for process technicians. Through its BASF contact, Bidwell has been assured full access to the Texas experience. Meanwhile, Benzing and Strickland recently explored with Pennsylvania State University at Erie the potential for jointly developing the polymer technician program. Both BASF and Penn State have been extremely helpful in determining equipment needs, instructional processes, and curriculum design. This next phase of collaboration, inasmuch as it involved greater organizational complexity, higher levels of resources, and new partners, moved the Bayer-Bidwell alliance further along the Collaboration Continuum. As the alliance network expands and more organizations become involved in such collaborations, ever greater social and economic value is created.

Shared Visioning

Having examined how the process of collaborating can lead incrementally and organically to additional cooperative activities, we now consider how partners' collective capacity to envision ever more enriching and powerful engagement opportunities can accelerate and extend alliance development.

Alan Khazei, for example, observed that City Year has "been able to go the furthest and develop the deepest partnership with Timberland because we both share this vision of a new paradigm of how business and community relate and how you can do well by doing good." And Michael Brown commented that "it was very clear to Timberland that City Year wanted to be the kind of organization that was on the cutting edge of engaging the private sector and saw all the value of full-scale engagement. And Timberland wanted to do the same with the nonprofit sector. Neither looked at philanthropy in a traditional or narrow way."

Finding future fit is critical to the ongoing strengthening of an alliance. It is natural and desirable to become intensely involved in current collaborative activities, but partners should periodically engage in a joint process of brainstorming about future collective efforts. Knowing what you've been able to accomplish together to date, what new collaborative terrain can you cover? What will be the next big leap for the alliance? What new combination of competencies and resources will produce big partnering payoffs? Creating a shared vision of the future is a powerful vehicle for engaging leadership and motivating organizations.

Achieving Environmental Fit

This discussion so far has emphasized the fit between partners. There is, however, another type of fit that must be kept in mind in strategy formulation. An effective strategy must also fit its environment so as to be able to effectively deal with external threats and capitalize optimally on contextual opportunities. Strategic alliances must also meet this environmental fit criterion.

Sometimes cross-sector alliances do not make sense because the partners' strategies are incompatible. Strategic misfits, however, may be transformed into strategic collaborators. This may occur, for example, when organizations' prevailing, conflict-inducing strategies are reformulated. Such strategic rethinking often is due to environmental shifts that make existing strategies obsolete and call for new visions. The subsequent reshaping is generally propelled by CEOs, particularly new ones who bring a different perspective. Independently reconfigured strategies might create new common ground for collaboration.

It is important that strategic thinkers understand the dynamics of environmental fit, the risk of strategy obsolescence, the task of strategy reformulation, and implications of creating strategic alliances. As The Nature Conservancy–Georgia-Pacific alliance provides a rich example of these phenomena, I end the chapter with a closer examination of that relationship, which converted combatants into collaborators.

Competing Agendas

Interactions between TNC and Georgia-Pacific date back more than two decades. Early interactions between the two organizations typically took the form described by Alex Hopkins, a Georgia-Pacific group manager and a key player in the company's recent landmark agreement to jointly manage lands in North Carolina with TNC: "Over twenty years ago, Georgia-Pacific worked with The Nature Conservancy and the state of Georgia to negotiate a below-market sale of Lewis Island, a six-thousand-acre island at the mouth of a major river. This type of transaction is typical of our past cooperative efforts with environmental and conservation groups. We negotiated agreements to sell or donate properties that they had deemed as high-priority sites for preservation."

Typically, such land was not highly productive for Georgia-Pacific, and the sale or donation was rationalized as providing a one-time public relations opportunity and some possible tax benefits. Recalled John Rasor, "Twenty years ago, I didn't think Georgia-Pacific had much in common with a group like The Nature Conservancy. We met with them and listened to them and then went back to work, but my opinion—back then—was that business and environmental groups had very little in common, and it was difficult to find the value in working together."

At this stage of their relationship the organizations had seemingly competing agendas. TNC's strategy was to acquire and protect from the "bad corporate giants" as much land as possible. Georgia-Pacific's was to manage land for maximum timber production. These environmental and economic goals were perceived to be in conflict. TNC acted offensively and pursued land acquisition and Georgia-

Pacific reacted defensively to environmental issues either by donating (outright or through below-market sales) selected lands, usually of low commercial value, or by simply refusing to deal with the petitions. If a deal could be struck, the value proposition was simple: TNC acquired land at below-market rates from the company, and Georgia-Pacific earned a public relations bonus and possibly a tax break. Because low-producing lands were the subject of the sale or donation, the business cost of the donation to Georgia-Pacific was minimal. As in most traditional philanthropic relationships, value transfer was predominantly one-way—the corporate partner was the primary giver and the nonprofit the receiver. Of little strategic importance to either organization, the majority of these transactions were negotiated at the local level, with little corporate guidance or involvement. This initial stage could thus be characterized as a sporadic, peripheral, deal-based relationship with philanthropic overtones, set against discernible antipathy and tension.

Strategy Obsolescence and Reexamination

As environmental and timber organizations such as TNC and Georgia-Pacific continued to pursue their independent agendas, the marketplace and political climate were changing. "As an industry we are currently facing unprecedented pressures," remarked Georgia-Pacific's Alex Hopkins. "We are challenged with managing our commercial forest lands in an environmentally sound way without compromising our competitive position in a global market for forest products." The environmental agenda has long been pursued through the regulatory process, and timber companies are now subject to strict and growing regulation. More than fifty thousand pieces of environmental legislation have been passed at the local, state, and federal levels. The conflict in the Pacific Northwest regarding the management of national forests and protection of the spotted owl increased public awareness about the clash between the economic goals of forest products companies and the environmental goals of conservation groups. For TNC, the accelerating pressures of urban, suburban, industrial, and rural development were rapidly out-pacing its efforts to conserve land. Ecosystems were being shredded.

TNC eventually recognized the limits of its strategy: it could never achieve on its own its goal of locking up all the endangered land and throwing away the key to commercial use. Its land acqui-sition resources paled in comparison to the vast areas that needed protection. The breadth and complexity of ecosystems extended far beyond the preserves it could ever control. TNC's traditional land conservation strategy was exhausted.

At the same time, Georgia-Pacific began to recognize the short-falls in its defensive strategy. When it sells or donates ecologically significant land, the company gives up two things: it loses access to that resource, and it realizes no lasting public relations value or long-term credibility. "These types of relationships are short-term in nature and do not necessarily build understanding and trust between the two groups," observed Alex Hopkins. And senior communica-tions manager Lynn Klein commented on the limits of Georgia-Pacific's traditional relations with environmental groups: "Usually when we sold land I felt that the underlying message was 'property saved from corporate giant.' We may have owned and managed the property for timber production for many, many years, but as soon as you transferred ownership you were not necessarily given credit for anything. You might get a brief mention in an article." Georgia-Pacific's strategy for dealing with the environment was yielding little.

New Leadership and New Strategies

Concurrent with changes in the marketplace and political climate, new leadership in both organizations sparked a shift in philosophy and strategy. A change in top leadership is often an opportunity for alliance creation, although it can also put existing alliances at risk. The new leaders at TNC and Georgia-Pacific chose to reformulate their obsolete core strategies to better fit external pressures in their respective environments. These strategy shifts also meant that cross-sector alliances became an attractive strategic tool.

When he took the helm at TNC in 1990, John Sawhill brought decades of experience in the business sector as a partner with McKinsey & Company, in the public sector as a government policymaker, and in the social sector as president of a major university. "Before I arrived," he recalled, "there was certainly an effort to reach out to the corporate community. I tried to accelerate the process. One of the things I did was to bring more CEOs onto our board to give us more credibility in the corporate community and to get their thinking about ways to work effectively with them. Secondly, we had talked about working with corporations, but frankly what that really meant was raising money from corporations. What we've tried to do in the last few years has been to develop partnerships where we're actually doing things together to accomplish conservation."

The leadership change also brought new attitudes and programs. After recognizing that its strategy of preservation through land acquisition could never achieve the needed massive conservation, TNC introduced in 1991 The Last Great Places, a systematic, science-based program to protect large, natural communities and preserve outstanding remaining ecosystems in the United States, Latin America, and the Pacific. The program establishes natural habitats within a managed landscape, surrounded by buffer zones used more intensively for economic, recreational, and other human activities. It was this program, which demonstrated TNC's commitment to both environmental and economic goals, that piqued Georgia-Pacific's interest in TNC.

Sawhill explained TNC's strategic shift this way:

> The number of partnerships has accelerated recently. This reflects a change in The Nature Conservancy's strategy. In the 1970s and into the 1980s, we thought the best way to go about our work was to go out and buy a piece of land and that way we could make sure it was protected. We began to realize that we had to think on

more of a landscape scale, and we had to try to convince other landowners to manage their lands in ways that would be consistent with our objectives. This has given rise to a lot more partnerships, because we realize that's the only way we can get these landscapes protected, and if we don't protect the landscapes we're not going to protect the biodiversity. A reorientation of our mission and strategy has led us into a much more aggressive partnership effort.

Pete Correll, when he assumed the role of CEO at Georgia-Pacific in 1993, inherited an organization consistently rated at the bottom of environmental stewardship charts. Recognizing that the old approach of confrontation with environmentalists was no longer a viable strategy, given the growing support for environmentalism among the public and the government, he made the environment a corporate priority. He defined environmental stewardship at Georgia-Pacific for both manufacturing and forestry operations; made a public statement about environmental stewardship in the new corporate vision; and hired Lee Thomas, former administrator of the federal Environmental Protection Agency, to lead the company's environmental effort. According to Rob Olszewski, "Lee was on a pretty strong mission to bring some visibility and some readjustment of our goals with consideration towards environmental concerns, and I think Pete gave him a pretty strong charge."

Under Correll and Thomas's guidance, Georgia-Pacific began to play an active role in defining environmental stewardship for a commercial forest, through both company and industrywide efforts. It adopted its eleven-point Forest Resources Environmental Strategy and played an instrumental role in the industrywide Sustainable Forestry Initiative. Olszewski's perspective on Georgia-Pacific's shift in strategy was that "we can't be a company that apologizes for managing intensely—that's our business and that's what generates the revenue for our shareholders. But I think our piece of the pie is recognizing that we do have some unique sites, and managing those appropriately where we do." Regarding the strategic shift that paved the way for the Lower Roanoke River agreement, Lynn Klein remarked: "It was the right time, industrywide and also within the company, to define environmental stewardship and figure out how we wanted to position ourselves environmentally."

Such changes in announced strategy were made credible by concrete actions undertaken by both Georgia-Pacific and TNC that facilitated the shift toward collaboration. Executives from both sides were receptive to the Roanoke proposal because they had seen concrete evidence of, not merely lip service to, a commitment to a new vision. Georgia-Pacific had been successful in its recent conservation efforts. Its agreement to manage an endangered species with the U.S. Fish and Wildlife Service provided a reference point and demonstrated the company's leadership position in endangered species management. TNC had evidenced its commitment to economic viability in its Last Great Places program. As Klein observed, "One of the things that prompted us to look at doing something different is the nature of TNC's Last Great Places program. It is not just a straight preservation program. In fact, what they're looking for is protection of ecosystems but also protection of economic activity. The view is that if you can protect the environment but still sustain the economic viability, then you have the best of both worlds—and that seems to be a big, big emphasis with Sawhill." And John Rasor contrasted TNC to other environmental groups: "TNC was not an advocacy group. The Environmental Defense Fund, in contrast, was suing forest companies, so we couldn't partner with them."

As Georgia-Pacific and TNC began to reposition themselves—the former with respect to environmental conservation and the latter with respect to economic use of natural resources—the stage was set for a more strategic and equal partnership. Each organization began to see the value in working with rather than against the other to accomplish organizational goals.

The Conversion to Collaboration

In late 1993, as the foregoing changes were taking effect, executives of Georgia-Pacific and TNC met to discuss potential land acquisition and protection projects. This meeting, different from any previous meeting between the two, marked the beginning of the landmark Lower Roanoke River project. "Right after Lee Thomas became the head of Georgia-Pacific's environmental group, we asked them if we could sit down and review a whole range of projects with them," recalled Sawhill. "It was a proactive effort on our part to go to them and say, 'You're a large landowner. There are a number of places where we want to work with you. Let's see if we can sit down and prioritize these things together.'" In effect, TNC had to restart its conversation with Georgia-Pacific, based on very different premises from its previous, more confrontational or deal-oriented, negotiating stance.

Georgia-Pacific asked TNC staff to "pitch" land acquisition or protection projects on company-owned forest land of high interest to TNC. At a meeting at the top of the Georgia-Pacific tower in downtown Atlanta, TNC proposed projects for a site in Arkansas, the Lower Roanoke River in North Carolina, and the Altamaha River in Georgia. "We developed a very rough list where there might be potential to work together on something," recalled Olszewski. "There was not a lot of clear definition when we left the room on that first day." Concurred Klein, "We didn't even have an idea of what we might do."

After that executive meeting, representatives from the relevant TNC state chapters returned home to meet with local Georgia-Pacific forestry personnel in order to develop proposals for management review. In North Carolina, Alex Hopkins and TNC's local representative, Fred Annand, led the proposal development effort.

Hopkins recalled that "at our first meeting in Raleigh, there was a certain level of mutual distrust. But from the outset we agreed to be open and honest about our objectives, our expectations, and our concerns. At the meeting we discussed pursuing other options instead of selling or donating the land." To engage in an effective joint discovery process of strategic fit, both organizations had to change qualitatively and fundamentally the nature of their dialogue and previous premises for cooperation.

After many discussions, Hopkins and Annand proposed to a combined meeting of the Georgia-Pacific and TNC leadership that the two organizations jointly manage twenty-one thousand acres of unique forested wetlands along North Carolina's Lower Roanoke River. The project called for the development of an ecosystem management plan to guide both conservation of this property designated a Last Great Place by TNC and ecologically compatible resource management, including timber management. The proposal was approved by the organizations' directors to resounding applause.

In Washington, D.C., on November 14, 1994, John Sawhill, Pete Correll, and Secretary of the Interior Bruce Babbitt conducted a press conference to announce the land management agreement. Such high public visibility signaled the strategic importance of the alliance to the partners. The Georgia-Pacific/The Nature Conservancy Ecosystems Partnership agreement includes the following elements:

- Georgia-Pacific's role. Georgia-Pacific is responsible for the ownership, operation, upkeep, and maintenance of the properties, including all associated costs, and for jointly developing and monitoring the ecosystem management plan.

- The Nature Conservancy's role. TNC is responsible for protecting the properties; monitoring and managing plant and animal populations, plant communities, and natural habitats; and jointly developing the ecosystem management plan. TNC will be given all hunting rights and, in the event of ownership transfer, have right of first refusal on a purchase of the land.

- Ecosystem management plan. This plan will ensure the highest level of conservation, and, if compatible, timber production. Timber harvesting is prohibited within 660 feet of the channel of any permanent stream or estuary, and all timber will have to be removed by helicopter (the environmentally least damaging method, albeit four times more costly).

- Land management team. The ecosystem management plan was developed and is managed by the Georgia-Pacific/The Nature Conservancy Ecosystems Partnership, which met quarterly through 1995 and continues to meet periodically. Members of the team include representatives from the North Carolina Wildlife Resources Commission, U.S. Fish and Wildlife Service, North Carolina State University Department of Forestry, Georgia-Pacific, and TNC (only the latter two groups have voting privileges).

This agreement was a dramatic departure from the traditional deals negotiated between Georgia-Pacific and TNC. First, it was not a deal, and second, it was not negotiated. More than a one-time date, the agreement is a commitment to a long-term relationship, the terms of which are set jointly by the partners. Each party brought scientific capabilities and resources that were of value to the other, thus creating a more equal value exchange.

The agreement also set a precedent for future collaboration. In Brunswick, Georgia, TNC conducted a three-day training session for Georgia-Pacific foresters on identifying unique native plant communities so these species could be protected. Declared Olszewski: "We both look at this as a neat pilot."

Strategic shifts have brought TNC and Georgia-Pacific, once positioned at opposite ends of the environmental-economic continuum, toward the middle, resulting in overlapping objectives. Given shared objectives, each organization invests in the relationship for its own strategic purposes, thereby creating a mutually reinforcing partnership. A personal connection with the social purpose, which was found to be a vital motivating factor in other alliances, appears to be less significant in this case. For Georgia-Pacific the driver seems to be primarily the perceived business strategy imperative of shifting to a more proenvironment approach so as to avoid or reduce onerous government regulation. Although the corporate executives have an increased recognition of the social merits of conservation, that cause does not seem to carry the high passion found in other social purpose alliances. Analogously, the TNC officials are sympathetic to but do not seem passionate about the social desirability of economically sustainable environmentalism. For both organizations their connection appears to be more instrumental than emotional. This does not seem to have impeded the alliance's development, however, probably because of its high relevance to the organizations' missions and the favorable personal relationships that have evolved. Over time, with greater interaction, the personal emotional connection may grow as well.

The sustainability of the alliance rests most fundamentally on its fit with the partners' reformulated strategies, which in turn represent a basic strategic realignment with their changing operating environments. Context is constantly changing, and effective strategies, including cross-sector collaborations, require ongoing adjustments.

Conclusion

Getting strategic fit right is a foundational task. Investing significant effort up front to align mission, strategy, and values pays off in alliance strength and sustainability. Formulating a partnership purpose and fit statement can help partners clarify their objectives and assess congruency. Meshing of missions may come easily in many instances but often requires digging to discover a common purpose and institutional fit. After an alliance becomes central to both partners' core strategies and missions, one big payoff is that it is more likely to weather transitory storms that might afflict one or the other partner. Sometimes alignment is achieved by matching the specific operating needs and capabilities of a business and NPO. When a clear business need is being met, corporate resources are more readily mobilized. Compatibility of organizational values creates cohesion and comprehension. In the integrative stage each organization's values can be significantly shaped by the other organization.

Strategic alliances are not instantaneous creations. They evolve through sequential acts of collaboration. Growing confidence and partnering expertise lead to broader and more significant joint activities. Partnering fosters learning, which in turn facilitates cooperation with other partners, thereby generating a collaboration multiplier effect. As well as aligning current strategies, missions, and values, partners should work to create future fit. Envisioning an alliance's next collaboration frontier energizes the partners and guides their continued effort to ensure strategic fit. NPOs and businesses face continually changing environments that can lead to changes in strategy. Such shifts may even create opportunities to convert past opponents into future collaborators. Yesterday's misfits can become tomorrow's collaborators in today's alliance marketplace.

5

Generating Value

Achieving strategic fit ensures that two organizations will mesh, but the more critical question that should be continually asked is, What is the collaboration's value to each partner? Every relationship involves an exchange of value among the participants. The magnitude, form, source, and distribution of that value is at the heart of relational dynamics. The perceived worth of an alliance is the ultimate determinant of, first, whether it will be created and, second, whether it will be sustained. It is thus important that partners be able to assess carefully the potential and actual value of collaborative activities.

Managers can systematically assess an alliance's value to the partners by means of the Collaboration Value Construct. The four dimensions of this basic framework are value definition, value creation, value balance, and value renewal. Examining these four dimensions reveals answers to the following basic questions about an alliance's worth:

- What does value mean to each of the partners?
- How do the partners create value for one another?
- How can partners keep a two-way balance in the exchange of values?
- What can be done to preserve and enrich the alliance's value?

This chapter examines each of these questions in terms of the key issues that surround the tasks of defining, creating, balancing, and renewing value.

Defining Value

To determine the value of a potential collaboration, the partners should first set clear expectations about what they want from the relationship. They should then try to quantify the benefits and weigh them against whatever costs might be incurred.

Setting Expectations

It is important that partners be clear about their mutual goals for collaboration. They should identify the multiple possible benefits accruing to each. As was mentioned in Chapter One, partnering benefits for nonprofits might include financial resources, services or goods, technical expertise and technologies, access to other corporations, enhanced name recognition, and new perspectives. Benefits for corporations might include improved image, higher employee morale, recruiting of more desirable job candidates, increased retention, skill development, product innovations, increased consumer patronage and market share, and enrichment of corporate values and culture.

It is also important to assess benefits to the larger society. The social value generated by collaboration will vary greatly with the social purpose. That purpose will generally be related primarily to the nonprofit's mission, but of particular interest is the incremental or distinctive social value created by the collaboration, in contrast to the partners individually. In effect, partners are asking how society is better off because of their joining of resources and efforts.

A Merck official stressed that "the expectations about what the partnership should produce have to be really clearly thought through on both sides before the partnership begins." A spokesperson for Merck's partner, The College Fund, coincided: "Sit down with the upper echelon in the company and set goals. Analyze the strengths and weaknesses of the partnership. Figure out a way to maximize those strengths and you can't lose. That all needs to be done up front." A staff member from Beginning with Children suggested that starting with "a full consideration of what all sides need" is the basis for a successful partnership. An MCI WorldCom manager explained, "We go through a very rigorous process when we choose our partners. We actually co-develop the proposal with them." Clarity of expectations is critical.

In effect, these organizations are suggesting that the development of the Collaboration Value Construct be a joint and highly participatory process that begins with a clear definition of what each side seeks from the partnership. To prevent nonprofits from overcommitting, United Way of Seattle advises them to conduct a capabilities analysis, to ensure that their competencies and resources match their partners' expectations. If the analysis uncovers a capabilities gap, it is advisable to adjust expectations downward, so as to avoid disappointment later, or to close the gap by acting to increase the nonprofit's competency.

The viability of an alliance depends fundamentally on its ability to create added value for both participants. This core relational premise anchors the relationship between Timberland and City Year. As City Year cofounder Michael Brown puts it: "Timberland is helping build City Year, but City Year is helping build Timberland." Timberland vice president of social enterprise Ken Freitas concurs: "That level of expectation and engagement is a fundamental part of our relationship."

The more clearly one can define the value expected from a collaboration, the better one can configure the alliance to produce it. This is well illustrated by the alliance of The Nature Conservancy (TNC) and Georgia-Pacific. As described earlier, in previous collaborations Georgia-Pacific had sold or donated land to conservation organizations, receiving in exchange the public relations and tax value of partnering with a credible nonprofit organization.

Moreover, both TNC and Georgia-Pacific still have various cause-related marketing arrangements with other organizations. These are tightly and contractually circumscribed transactional relationships. However, in their alliance, Georgia-Pacific and TNC were seeking a higher level of engagement in order to produce a different kind of benefit. Explained Georgia-Pacific senior vice president John Rasor: "We did not want to just donate the land. Our continued involvement was important so that we could demonstrate our ability for proactive landscape management. Partnerships provide us with the third-party endorsement we need in order to be viewed as good environmental stewards. It becomes part of our 'proof of performance' approach to validating our company's environmental commitments and goals."

Quantifying Benefits

The more specifically and quantitatively managers can articulate the expected benefits to partners and to society, the greater guidance the collaboration will have. Moreover, the funding community in general is increasingly looking for organizations to measure and demonstrate results from funders' social investments. Although value assessments often cannot be quantified with precision, these qualitative statements are also valuable and legitimate. Whatever the benefit indicators are, they must be deemed useful and convincing to the relevant stakeholders in each organization if the alliance is to garner the internal support needed to sustain it. Additionally, as discussed later in this chapter, each organization needs to weigh these benefits against the costs and risks of collaborating to determine the advisability of proceeding.

The value of collaboration to a nonprofit is ultimately expressed as a sum of money or quantity of in-kind resources that a company provides in exchange for the nonprofit's services or, for example, the use of its name in a cause-related marketing transaction. This value is a key determinant of whether or not the collaboration is worth undertaking. In effect it is the *price* of or the amount of the *invest-*

ment in the collaboration. Setting this price is often a complicated task. As one nonprofit executive commented: "The most difficult piece of advice to give is the one we keep asking ourselves, which is, 'What price do we put on our involvement in these campaigns?' . . . Every day the phone is ringing and ideas are coming in unsolicited. It may be $10,000 to be part of a product promotion, or $50,000 or $500,000. The nonprofit has to be able to set priorities and be able to say, 'It's worth this amount.'"

Part of the problem is that managers have no place in the underdeveloped alliance marketplace to find the going price for, say, the use of a nonprofit's name. Managers do not have large numbers of alliances to which to refer, and where alliances have occurred, transaction details are not necessarily public. Moreover, each partnership transaction deals with assets peculiar to the specific partners and consequently not necessarily applicable to another set of partners. However, when managers are dealing with more than one potential partner, they can compare how much each might offer for the partnering arrangement. They might also consult with another known and similar NPO or corporation that has engaged in alliances to obtain a reference point.

TNC president John Sawhill explained that

> We price based on what the market will bear and what our time and effort are worth. There is increased competition. There's a lot of choices out there. You have to stay constantly on your toes and increase the value of your package to the corporation. We talk about our reach through our membership and the strength of our brand, which we're not particularly scientific about measuring. But we talk about how long we've been in existence, how many field offices we have, and other proxies like that. You literally build up a set of benefits, such as exposure in our magazine, invitations to various events, rights to use the logo in certain marketing campaigns,

rights to buy our membership list, and then price each component. We're finding increasingly that the more specific we get about pricing, the more attractive the proposal becomes.

Another complication is that the benefits that accrue to nonprofits may extend beyond the financial and in-kind resources received, which are relatively easy to quantify. Interactions with their corporate partners frequently enrich their perspectives, management skills, organizational systems, and marketing. A Reading Is Fundamental executive stressed the benefit of enhanced visibility, saying, "For the nonprofit, reputation is close to being everything. And reputation is closely tied to visibility. Your reputation is enhanced not just by the good work you do but by the recognition you get for doing it. So the relationship that helps us get the word out about the organization is important. It's hard to put a dollar value on it. It's important not just for the branding effort of a national nonprofit organization, but it's also important for the local volunteers in the field who absolutely love to feel a part of something big and important."

Surveyed nonprofits also cite increased access to other corporations as valuable. A National Geographic Society spokesperson noted that "we've had lots of good press. Many other companies and foundations are taking notice." These benefits are real but, again, difficult to quantify.

Corporations wrestle with this valuation problem too. Georgia-Pacific faced the challenge of convincing internal skeptics about the value of its relationship with TNC. "There are some folks who are pretty hard-core business folks who challenge the issue," observed Director of Environmental Affairs Rob Olszewski. "It is very difficult to quantify the business benefits of the partnership to your organization in traditional means. These are people who tend to be very straight finance-oriented people who probably would not think as broadly as a Pete Correll would. If you're not willing to think a little broader, you can raise some questions about partnerships like this."

Timberland, likewise, faced the challenge of convincing internal skeptics and external stock analysts that its investment in City Year made business sense. Quantifying benefits in the areas of employee morale, commitment, recruitment, retention, leadership development, team building, and brand enhancement, like quantifying the bottom-line benefits of advertising or management training programs, remains difficult. Internal support was strained when Timberland incurred losses and had to downsize. Outlays to City Year were hard for employees to take when colleagues were losing their jobs. Yet making the Collaboration Value Construct work for internal and external stakeholders is a perpetual challenge that must be met, because the viability of an alliance ultimately depends on demonstrating its value to key constituencies through quantitative, qualitative, and experiential evidence.

As the alliance marketplace matures, valuation and pricing will become easier. This is happening at an accelerating rate in cause-related marketing collaborations, which constitute perhaps the fastest growing segment of corporate advertising. Many businesses and nonprofits view these alliances as relatively narrow and sharply focused transactions. Measures used in advertising—such as audience size, location, and demographics—are being used to assess and attach value to them. The growing systematization of the valuation process is helpful, but there is the risk that the search for more easily quantifiable forms of collaboration will lead to alliance myopia. The more multifaceted collaboration configurations in the transactional and integrative stages, although more difficult to value, might have greater strategic worth.

Recognizing Costs

Valuation consists of weighing benefits against costs. A natural and important concern of each partner entering an alliance is the effect the relationship might have on its name. Reputational risk impeded some of the early collaboration initiatives between Timberland and City Year.[1] "When we tried to do the advertising program initially with City Year," reported Freitas, "they refused, saying, 'No, that's not us; it's the wrong kind of thing.' It takes time to get past these initial, what are perceived as unnatural, things." Timberland COO Jeff Swartz recounted Michael Brown's objection—"You are commercializing something that is sacred"—and subsequent retrospective reassessment—"Looking back on it now, I think we were oversensitive to our brand." The risk and concern declined over time, in part because the two partners developed greater trust and understanding. Fear of being exploited diminished and a reassessment of the risk exposure yielded a different conclusion.

Association nevertheless incurs a mutual assumption of risk. Each partner may be held accountable for the behavior of the other. When, for example, Timberland was accused of environmentally damaging waste disposal practices in an overseas factory, City Year's leaders were criticized for their affiliation. Similarly, when the *Boston Globe* published an article highly critical of City Year, many questioned Timberland's partnership. Swartz expressed the challenge this way: "You are aware that people will throw stones, and even some windows may be broken, but you are deeply committed. How do you work through those risks? The way you work through risks in a marriage. Each bears the other's sins." And you try to help the partner deal with the situation. In response to the *Globe* article, for example, Timberland and City Year's other corporate sponsors rallied behind City Year, demonstrating their endorsement and providing technical assistance to strengthen City Year's administrative systems. The net results were a healthier organizational apparatus for City Year and a subsequent *Globe* editorial supporting City Year.

Because City Year and Timberland had the strength of mutual commitment that characterizes integrative stage relationships, they could weather controversy and even protect each other's reputations. Staying power is less when a relationship is in the philanthropic stage or is a narrow, cause-related marketing deal in the transactional stage. Witness the highly publicized collapse of the alliance between the American Medical Association and Sunbeam Corporation. The AMA had entered into a five-year cause-related marketing agreement that gave its "seal of approval" to Sunbeam products in return for "royalties." When this staff-initiated agreement became public, it met with criticism from some AMA members and surprise from the AMA board members, who had not approved the deal, leading the AMA to cancel the agreement. The exit cost to the AMA was a damage and legal fees payment to Sunbeam of $9.9 million, and several AMA staff were fired.[2] The urge to capture new revenue streams should not blind an organization to its need to ensure that collaboration is consistent with its mission and acceptable to the primary stakeholders.

When Allen Grossman was CEO of Outward Bound, he rejected a commercial relationship in which Outward Bound would endorse a sportswear company's products, basing his action on the following reasoning:

> It is not that our name is holy; however, it does stand for specific principles and values that we have diligently promoted in the U.S. over the past thirty years—service, trust, community, self-esteem, etc. Can any product stand for the fundamental objectives of our organization, the essence of our being? A successful advertising campaign might generate substantial revenues in the short term, but it could easily change the public's perception of our organization. The obvious risk is disassociating our name from our mission. Our name would become someone else's marketing tool and by carefully crafted design, become identified with a product or company rather than our values. I don't think our name can stand for both. The comfortable exceptions are products like T-shirts, mugs, hats, knives, etc. The Outward Bound name on these kinds of products celebrates our existence,

has ample precedent with similar nonprofits, and is, I
believe, perceived by the public as just good fun and
internally produced advertising.

Cause-related marketing agreements are coming under closer
scrutiny by state attorneys general, some of whom have successfully
sued a handful of companies for advertisements that falsely implied
product endorsements by NPOs. SmithKline Beecham, for example,
settled for $2.5 million against the claim that Nicoderm advertise-
ments carrying the American Cancer Society name and logo and the
phrase "partners in helping you quit" made consumers believe the
society had endorsed the product.[3] These examples suggest that both
companies and NPOs need to exercise careful judgement in the
design of cause-related advertising. The attorneys general are pushing for regulatory guidelines that will require company advertisements using an NPO's name to state that there is no endorsement if
none has been formally given, disclose that the NPO is receiving
payment for the use of its name if that is the case, and state whether
the relationship with the NPO is exclusive.

What can cloud managers' judgment is that the potential rewards
of cause-related marketing deals are high. In 1998, nonprofits
received $1.5 billion in marketing fees, five times more than they
had taken in ten years earlier.[4] The Boys and Girls Clubs of America signed a $60 million, ten-year agreement that will put Coca-Cola
vending machines in the two thousand clubs.[5] The clubs' senior vice
president of marketing observed: "The debate is over whether cause-
related marketing is a good thing or not. Those standing back are
going to watch the world march right on by." The American Heart
Association has generated millions of dollars from its certification of
more than six hundred products as "heart healthy."[6] A national survey has indicated that 76 percent of the public believe it is appropriate for companies to undertake cause-related marketing and that
they would switch to a brand associated with a good cause if price
and quality were equal to those of other brands.[7] This form of col-

laboration can produce significant benefits for both partners, but care must be taken to not mislead consumers or violate the organization's mission.

A TNC executive in charge of cause-related marketing recounted how that nonprofit addresses the management of this risk:

> We have to make sure from the beginning of a relationship that our goals are closely enough aligned that when we come out with a marketing communications message it works for us and for the corporation. We also govern the use of our brand through contract and through some ongoing management of the relationship. Part of what Canon USA, for example, perceives that they're getting is the right to use our trademarks and talk about us in their marketing efforts. As long as we have some control over how our trademarks appear and how our image is used, we're very interested in having them take advantage of that right, because it's garnered us millions and millions of exposures in media that we could never hope to purchase for ourselves.

The executive also pointed out that another possible cost arises when a corporation fails to fully promote the relationship after it has been given an exclusive right in its category. TNC then gets cash for the right but none of the hoped-for exposure. Underexposure can be a cost just as misexposure can.

Among other costs that should also be taken into the benefit-cost calculation are the incremental demands that will be placed on what is often an organization's scarcest resource, leadership time. Managers need to weigh the opportunity costs of the resources to be mobilized. Because resource demands generally increase as an alliance progresses along the Collaboration Continuum, incremental benefits must also become greater. Partners should discuss explicitly how to reduce the costs and manage the risks of moving to another stage in their alliance.

Creating Value

Defining expected benefits to each partner clarifies mutual understanding and frames the partners' joint hopes, but the core task is the creation of that value. Managers must identify how the partners' resources can be mobilized to generate value. This may be better understood by recognizing that different types of resources produce different magnitudes of benefit. This section examines three types of resource mobilization: transfer of generic resources, exchange of core capabilities, and joint creation of value. It also looks at another important way to multiply value—through multiparty alliances.

Source and Magnitude

Partnerships are strengthened when the partners think continually about value creation, when they scrutinize each organization's resources and capabilities to see how they can be made to generate value. As a relationship progresses, the partners move beyond generic resource transfer and begin using their core capabilities and proprietary assets to generate benefits, thereby increasing their worth to the collaboration. At the higher relationship levels, partners should seek to synergistically combine their resources to jointly create benefits, a process that enhances the value of the collaboration because it produces benefits not otherwise attainable.

The magnitude of the value created is related to the nature of the resources deployed.

In a *generic resource transfer* each organization provides to the other benefits that derive from resources common to many similar organizations. For example, the company gives money to the nonprofit, and the nonprofit supplies good deeds and good feelings. Each lends credibility and image enhancement to the other in its respective sector. These types of mutual benefits are common in most philanthropic relationships. The nature of the resources transferred and benefits produced is not determined by specific characteristics of the partners.

In a *core competencies exchange* each institution's distinctive capabilities are used to generate the benefits to the partner and the collaboration. These benefit flows have greater potential value creation, because each organization is leveraging special competencies and providing proprietary or otherwise distinctive resources. The specific identify of each member of the partnership does make a difference to the type and level of benefits generated.

In *joint value creation* benefits are neither bilateral resource transfers nor exchanges but rather joint products or services derived from the combination of the organizations' competencies and resources. This is a particularly high-value source of benefits because it is unique to the alliance and thus not replicable by others.

Let's look further at each of these sources of value.

Generic Resource Transfer

The simplest and most common resource flow consists of company funds given to an NPO and goodwill returned to the corporation. This first-stage philanthropic engagement is important to NPO cash flow. There being an abundant literature, there is no need to elaborate on traditional fundraising techniques.[8] However, the observation of one CARE manager warrants attention: "As a nonprofit your lifeblood is your ability to secure donations and resources. You have to manage the duality of identifying where you can access those resources near term but also plant the seeds for longer-term relationships. You've got to be governed not by where you can generate the resources now but rather where having an alliance with a corporation can build into something that's greater than the two organizations."

Core Competencies Exchange

This type of exchange enhances an alliance's value to the partners because each provides more or less nonreplicable benefits.[9] For example, Timberland supplied with its boots and apparel its brand image, community service culture, visioning capabilities, employee volunteers, and corporate relationship network (for instance, it convinced its long-distance provider, MCI WorldCom, to provide discounted telephone service and its watch supplier, Timex, to donate watches to City Year). In turn, Timberland benefited from City Year's supplying its proprietary competencies in leadership and diversity training and service project management, its understanding of community relationships, its youth corps members as community workers and as job recruits, and its visioning ability. Timberland also gained government accolades for its association with the community service organization. President Clinton, being particularly impressed with City Year, modeled AmeriCorps on it. When the president convened a national conference on corporate community service, Timberland's association with City Year highlighted Timberland's community leadership on an equal footing with that of such corporate giants as Coca-Cola and IBM, an enormous public relations boost for the company.

To generate value for each other, partners must be willing to learn about one another's organizations. Swartz's participation on City Year's board has involved deep learning about the NPO. After City Year cofounder Alan Khazei attended Timberland's international salesforce conference, Jeff Swartz remarked: "Before you ask for anything you should learn what you can do for the other guy. Alan internalized that, and it's had a huge benefit. Timberland people think it's the coolest thing in the world that Alan understands the white-shoe to brown-shoe transformation occurring in our industry." And Khazei described how this kind of understanding helped him reformulate a request to Timberland for uniforms for a new middle school youth service initiative. Whereas the original request had emphasized the *do-good* aspect of the donation, the revised proposal employed brand marketing terms that enabled the Timberland people to see the connection between the donation and their company from their vantage point.

The value of the alliance between CARE and Starbucks emerged partially from their similar needs and complementary core capabilities. Both organizations needed to get their mission messages to the public. Characterizing the mutual benefit, one CARE manager said: "Starbucks was creating an image, an aura, a whole coffee experience. And that unique experience was not just a good cup of coffee but also 'we source from unique places all over the world and we do it in a respectful and humane way to the people we work with, just as we treat you, our customers, in a respectful way.' The linkage to CARE was another way of demonstrating and manifesting their vision so that the average customer coming into the store could appreciate it."

The relationship also provided CARE with a new avenue for getting out the message of how it helped people in developing countries. Daily exposure to thousands of Starbucks customers represented extraordinary coverage, well beyond CARE's possible access to other advertising media. As former CARE president Phil Johnston summed it up, "The Starbucks relationship was very, very valuable because it created a great deal of visibility for CARE with the general public, and creating visibility on your own dollar is very expensive. None of our other corporate alliances creates such visibility."

CARE regional director Peter Blomquist exuded enthusiasm over Starbucks' exclusive 1995 promotion in celebration of CARE's fiftieth anniversary: "You walked into a Starbucks store that month," he elaborated, "and there were banners hanging from the ceiling, a poster, T-shirts, mugs, all with CARE on them. There was a big stand-alone informational kiosk that had beautiful color pictures of each of the four CARE projects that Starbucks was supporting and an intelligent description of the project. For a nonprofit, this was a died-and-gone-to-heaven promotion from a highly visible, cool, fast-growing company. It was in some ways the culmination." In effect, Starbucks was leveraging its core competencies to create name recognition value for its partner and accompanying business value for itself. In the process the collaboration was educating the public about developing countries.

CARE in turn used its core competencies to design and operate the development projects supported by Starbucks. Its knowledge of the countries from which Starbucks sourced coffee, moreover, became a valuable company resource, giving Starbucks executives like Dave Olsen "a really reliable source of good information about current events politically, economically, socially, and environmentally."

Georgia-Pacific and The Nature Conservancy also exchange core competencies. TNC brings to the relationship an understanding of business not often found in a conservation group, a credible and solid reputation, and four hundred world-class scientists with knowledge of ecosystems such as the Lower Roanoke River. One Georgia-Pacific executive confided that even had the company been willing to undertake the Roanoke project itself, it would have been unable to do so without TNC's expertise. The alliance with TNC also gives Georgia-Pacific a seat at the table when environmental issues and solutions are being discussed.

For its part, Georgia-Pacific granted to TNC land of strategic conservation importance, access to its growing network of environmentally conscious timber companies, and also access to its huge knowledge of forest management. Additionally, Georgia-Pacific's publicizing of the partnership in national print media gained for TNC valuable name exposure that it could not otherwise have afforded. "As a membership organization," acknowledged John Sawhill, "we need to get better name recognition, so Georgia-Pacific's publicity is very valuable to us." These resource transfers enhance mission accomplishment and increase the mutual value of the collaboration.

Other collaborations surveyed also demonstrate how partners can leverage their core capabilities and resources. "Writing a check is often a convenient method to donate to charitable causes; however, using creativity to understand a nonprofit's needs can increase the strength of the donation," emphasized a Pfizer spokesperson. Pfizer provided its partner school with buildings, a science classroom, volunteer speakers, and a paid science curriculum developer. An MCI WorldCom executive stated, "I think the main reason for our success is that we don't just write a check. We are not believers in checkbook philanthropy; we put our resources behind the dollars." A Time Warner manager saw that company's literacy alliance as having evolved since 1985: "It is still a magazine-based program, but we also have open-captioned music videos, a newsroom, audio books, DC Comics. As our business has evolved, our program has evolved to reflect it. It moves as our business moves and where the business moves. It is a very strategic program for us." New capabilities mean new value opportunities.

Hewlett-Packard's grants of approximately $3 million and technical advice to the National Science Resources Center (NSRC) and forty-one school districts brought this observation from a company manager: "Every district I've talked to says, 'You know, your money was nice, but the biggest contribution you made was your people.'" NSRC remarked that Hewlett-Packard (HP) "has given us a whole fresh way of looking at what we're about. They have helped our communities utilize the principles of quality assessment and strategic planning. They have helped to raise our awareness and educate us about issues that we would never have thought of, like school-to-work. Ultimately this serves to increase the quality of our programs." As a credible, neutral party, HP was able to convene and foster exchanges among multiple educational district representatives that produced important lateral learning. This knowledge exchange was powerful because it leveraged the institutions' core capabilities.

Organizations should start expecting benefit exchanges to be bilateral. As a United Way of Seattle executive related: "Blake Nordstrom called me a month ago and said, 'We're looking at our community programs nationally. Can you help us?' We put a lot of work in on this and gave them some good recommendations. You have to be prepared to give that level of effort, because when you're in a close relationship, they will always be coming to you for advice." Even a historically philanthropic organization like the United Way is increasingly creating transactional and integrative relationships.

Joint Value Creation

Typically, the greatest value is generated when partners combine their capabilities synergistically, rather than simply transfer or exchange resources. The MarcoPolo Web site, for example, could not have been created by MCI WorldCom or National Geographic Society or any of the other partners alone. Only by combining their core competencies were these partners able to produce this educationally rich and powerful learning vehicle.

CARE and Starbucks were similarly able to generate novel benefits by combining CARE's traditional development expertise with the new knowledge Starbucks had gained from its collaboration with CARE. Olsen reported that in Guatemala, for example, "we're trying to apply our collective growing intelligence to make really strategic choices about the type and form of development projects." Another joint resource is the partnership model, as Blomquist said CARE discovered: "The model itself was and is of tremendous value to CARE. It was phenomenal for me to knock on the door of another business and say, 'Have you heard about what we're doing with Starbucks?' There was immediate receptivity and interest."

Georgia-Pacific and TNC are jointly demonstrating that forestry practices are compatible with important environmental functions and values. In addition to achieving economic and environmental goals, they are generating goodwill with both the public and government regulators, an important asset in land management. "We would like people to think of forestry as a legitimate land use, as one that is very low intensity and compatible with the environment," Olszewski emphasized. "The regulation of forest land management activities is still fairly subjective. As a result, I would attach some very high significance to the kinds of images you paint for your organization with agreements like this. When it comes down to a tough negotiating setting, I would not underestimate how they view us versus someone that they perceived as not being very concerned about environmental issues."

Bidwell Training Center, Bayer, and Sony's collaborative production of three CDs, one a Grammy award winner, was similarly possible only through the collective leveraging of their respective capabilities. Rather than a resource exchange, it was joint value creation. Strickland recounted the project's genesis:

> We were at the [Bayer] plant, and they took us over and showed us a laboratory that shows how Bayer uses its polycarbonate resin to make CDs. I'm thinking, "These guys got resin, I got music. There is a deal here someplace." I proposed that we take some of their plastic and put some of our music on it and see what would happen. Well, the long and short of the story is that we have three CDs out on the street. The first one that we made was a compilation of ten songs donated by the artists, including Dizzie Gillespie, entitled *Our New Home* in celebration of our new building.

Over the years, Strickland had developed good relationships with some African American musicians who were attracted to Bidwell's mission. Using these connections with the music industry, Bidwell sent the first recording out, and it quickly made the top twenty. Then the Count Basie Band came to town and, recalls Strickland, "The guys were so taken by this whole place that the band agreed to donate the concert as a way of giving a little something back to the community." Bidwell recorded the concert in its state-of-the-art auditorium, Sony pressed the CD with Bayer resin, and it won a Grammy. "Here are these high-tech companies partnering with a black and white community-based organization and winning a Grammy award for recording the Count Basie Orchestra," enthused Strickland. "Now, marketing people kill for opportunities like that. Our names were mentioned in every important newspaper in the United States of America, including the *New York Times*, *Chicago Tribune*, *L.A. Times*, and the *Detroit Free Press*. There's a partnership that is made in heaven!"

The collaboration also strengthened Bayer's supplier relationship with Sony. Historically a minor supplier of polycarbonate resin to Sony, Bayer was able to capitalize on its relationship with Bidwell to generate more business with the company. In combination, Bidwell and Bayer offered Sony not only resin but also a state-of-the-art recording venue and relationships with some of the country's leading jazz musicians. "This deal gave us access to some people," recalled a Bayer executive. "We still had to do all the normal things that you have to do and provide a quality product at the right price. But I think it did help to form a corporate relationship, and that's often the most difficult part of the job."

When partnerships migrate deeply into the second and third stages on the Collaboration Continuum, new organizational cultures are sometimes created. A United Way spokesperson observed that the United Way partnership with Nordstrom had reached the point where "our identities are interwoven." Other corporate partners surveyed cited image enhancement, brand building, employee recruiting assistance, and work enrichment as important benefits. For example, Reebok's award-winning work in human rights pervades its culture and has helped recruiting. "When people come to interview, the first thing they are going to do is to sign onto www.Reebok.com," explained a Reebok executive. "There is a human rights section on the Web site, and people come to Human Resources and indicate an interest in our company because of that."

"In the rating for best overall card, which is a key measure, we jumped seven share points after partnering with Reading Is Fundamental," recounted a spokesperson for Visa. Summing up, another corporate manager observed: "We have received wonderful benefits in working with our partners. And we wouldn't know about half the opportunities if we didn't have a true partnership. We wouldn't know about their distribution channels, their memberships. They have unbelievable assets, but they don't necessarily know how to exploit them all. When you work with them in a really close partnership, they will let you utilize those assets."

Multiparty Collaboration

Recognizing that the more partners, the greater the opportunities for synergistic activity, Hewlett-Packard actively pursues collaboration with other corporations as a way to mobilize additional and complementary resources. Explains an HP executive: "We happen to be able to give equipment, so we can give more value for the same after-tax cost. It's to our benefit to partner with someone who has cash to give and their benefit to partner with us. We both win." A manager of the National Geographic Society extolled the virtues of having multiple NPO partners in the MarcoPolo partnership: "They are all prestigious, established, and have means to do things that we can't do and have connections to the science folks, the historians, the artists, and all the rest."

As a particularly rich example of mobilizing multiple partners to generate value, the Bidwell-Bayer partnership warrants deeper exploration. Invited by retired Bayer vice president Peter Benzing to visit the Bidwell Training Center, Richard White, a friend of Benzing and a vice president at Bayer, was immediately convinced that the training program Bayer was considering was something more than a local opportunity, that it was a larger industry issue that warranted a broad coalition of collaborators. Strickland solicited county commissioner Tom Forester, a friend of Bidwell's, to cosign with White a letter to twenty-five companies proposing a program to train chemical technicians and requesting support to develop it. Seven of the companies—PPG Industries, Alcoa, Aristech Chemical, Calgon Carbon, Neville Chemical Company, Indspec Chemical Corporation, and Fisher Scientific—agreed to work with Bayer. The businesses defined this training program as a collaboration arena rather than territory for competition, and PPG Industries donated a senior research chemist to help teach and manage the course for two years.

In May 1990, in collaboration with the Pittsburgh Private Industry Council (PIC) and Bidwell, representatives of the collaborating companies began to meet on a regular basis to plan the chemical lab technician training program. That Bidwell had entered the initiative in alliance with Bayer facilitated the collaboration. An advisory committee explored the demand for lab technicians, identified internship opportunities, secured funding, and oversaw curriculum design. Strickland, recognizing that successful training requires hands-on involvement of operators, not personnel or human resource staff, recruited the PPG chemist as the instructor, who worked with lab tech supervisors to develop the curriculum.

By mid-fall 1990, the group had recruited and tested trainees, secured internship opportunities with the participating companies, and developed a year-long training program that satisfied industry needs for entry-level technicians. The forty-nine-week course of instruction covers the basics of organic, inorganic, and physical chemistry, with a strong emphasis on hands-on laboratory skills and safety. Additional monetary support was forthcoming in the form of a $76,500 grant from the Ben Franklin Technology Center of Western Pennsylvania, an $11,600 grant from the Spectroscopy Society of Pittsburgh, and $16,700 from the Bayer Corporation.

A year after its initiation, the program graduated sixteen students. Bidwell continued to offer the program, and the number of supporting companies doubled to fourteen. By 1998, according to Benzing, the program had graduated well over a hundred technicians. "It is an ongoing program," he emphasized. "The people find jobs. The program is now well known and the quality of the graduates is well known, so they are very much in demand."

Bayer and Bidwell recognized that they could not achieve their ambitious objectives alone, that the magnitude of this project dictated the support of other companies and the government. As lead company in the chemical technician training program, Bayer wisely constructed a multiparty alliance that was able to exploit synergies generated by the deployment of more and varied resources.

Bayer engages other partners not only to start programs but also to ensure sustainability, according to Bayer Foundation executive director Sande Deitch. "We always feel that we need to have partnerships when we start a program because, if you don't, and if Bayer were to hit on hard times or decide to change, then what you started would not continue."

Multiparty collaboration sometimes grows out of initial success in a two-party alliance, as illustrated by the evolution of the relationship between The Nature Conservancy and Georgia-Pacific. Their initial project on the Lower Roanoke River was a positive experience for both. But because the region had less timber value than many other Georgia-Pacific lands and was difficult to harvest, the risks to the company were manageable and far outweighed by potential gains from the collaboration. Said one Georgia-Pacific executive of what turned out to be an excellent first project in which to test new waters: "We would do this again even if it were the only deal, but it became foundational for us."

Building upon this foundation, the collaboration undertook in late 1998 a higher-stakes project in Georgia's Altamaha River region. The land, designated one of The Nature Conservancy's Last Great Places, has large industrial ownership and intensive forest management. "These are very productive timberlands coming to the table in this agreement," explained Olszewski, who is overseeing the project. "The hardwood sites on this property are generally quite better and more accessible than our Roanoke River sites. It's more of a real-life opportunity than Roanoke."

The Altamaha River project brought TNC and Georgia-Pacific together with two other forest product companies and the Georgia Department of Natural Resources (DNR). Under the agreement and the DNR's own River Care program, the DNR bought from the three companies the timber and development rights for the ecologically important three-hundred-foot-wide strip of riverfront for fifty miles of the river.[10] The companies retain title to their remaining thirty-seven thousand acres. For an initial period of five years the companies commit a portion of the funds paid by the DNR to help support research work in this floodplain area abutting the river.

The companies also commit for research the thirty-seven thousand acres to which they retain ownership.

To this deal the three companies bring the land base, DNR the money from its River Care program, and TNC the staff and expertise. Together the five organizations will form a steering committee that will direct the funding of the research projects. The research plan calls for a $100,000 annual budget, with the expectation that the project will attract matching funds. Georgia-Pacific and the other two companies will continue to operate and manage the land for forestry production, under a forest management plan.

Compared to the Roanoke project area, the Altamaha site offers much more favorable economics of timber management. Although partners to the agreement may withdraw at any point, they are agreed that a five-year period should be adequate to determine whether the time and financial commitments are beneficial and that the end of this period represents a logical point at which to reassess the provisions of the agreement.

Olszewski reported that the rationale for bringing in other companies as partners had several points: "In addition to the fact that we are looking at a more realistic multi-ownership landscape on the Altamaha, we're concerned about the image of the entire industry. If everybody feels like Georgia-Pacific, or only some segment of the industry, is the only one who is acting responsibly, a regulator could take the position that tough new restrictions are needed. And the industry is very diverse. There are reasons to broaden the partnership and get some additional leverage and also share some of the burdens of managing the project going forward—these things do require manpower and time."

As in the Bidwell-Bayer alliance, broadening the collaboration to a multiparty structure enabled project expansion, reduced the individual cost burden, and fostered a cooperative rather than competitive industry approach. However, it also made the task of defining value for the individual partners more complex.

Social Benefits

The value creation process of social purpose alliances generates incremental benefits not only to the partners but also to society. A stronger NPO does benefit society, but the benefits generated by an effective alliance often go beyond simply strengthening NPOs so that their social missions can be accomplished more effectively. This section samples numerous benefits that can accrue to society from collaborative relationships between corporations and NPOs.

The social value that has been generated by the City Year–Timberland alliance, for example, takes the form of significantly expanded community service, provided not only by City Year's youth corps but also by Timberland employees. It is doubtful that either organization alone could have achieved the current levels of service. Timberland's multifaceted support enabled City Year to scale up to a national level, and City Year's support and positive reinforcement facilitated Timberland's increases in the paid-time allocation for employee community service. Not only did the absolute number of person-days of community service provided by both organizations grow, but the quality of that service was enhanced by the mutual training and organizational strengthening the organizations provided to one another and developed together.

Moreover, to the extent that the personal enrichment and development of individual service providers (the employees and corps members) disposes them to continue to engage in community service and to be sensitive to individuals and institutions in need, the community's social capital and citizenship have been increased. The imprinting of the value of community service on youth corps members' personal value structures ensures society will enjoy a future stream of benefits as these individuals engage in other community betterment activities. Their experience with participating corporations, moreover, to the extent that it imparts a vision of the positive role business can play in social sector causes, can serve to reinforce such engagements.

Social purpose partnerships can also serve as motivating and informative models for others to follow. Social innovation relies on pioneers such as City Year and Timberland, both of which have generously and even proactively shared their experience with and encouraged other corporations and nonprofits.

The greater degree of land conservation attributable to the collaboration between TNC and Georgia-Pacific aids the preservation of biodiversity by preventing environmental degradation of valuable ecosystems, thereby enriching the public commons. Because the partnership targets at-risk zones, its payoff is particularly high relative to that of more generalized conservation efforts.

In the Lower Roanoke River project, the short-term environmental benefit is quantifiable in terms of habitat preservation. But the social value creation may more appropriately be seen as a stream of future conservation projects undertaken by the original partners both together and with others. The Altamaha project, which enlisted the support of a governmental agency and two other timber companies, is a case in point. The confidence and competency it gained through the Roanoke partnership led Georgia-Pacific to undertake the Florida project mentioned in the last chapter. Similarly, TNC, thanks to introductions made by Georgia-Pacific's CEO, is exploring analogous collaborations with other forest products companies. Societal benefits derive from the incremental preservation of ecosystems and from behavioral change on the part of the initiating partners and the other institutions they influence. The success of the alliance between Georgia-Pacific and TNC could precipitate a shift of scarce energies and resources away from traditionally confrontational engagements between conservation groups and timber companies toward more collaborative, conservation-oriented relationships.

CARE's alliance with Starbucks produced three types of societal benefits. First, greater resources were deployed to development projects in four countries. Second, thousands of consumers were made more aware of the situations and needs of people in developing countries, and this has contributed to greater global understanding and caring. Third, the partnership has served as a catalyst for other alliances, both between the originating partners and among observers of the partnership.

Time Warner cites the social value of improved literacy as the most important benefit of its cross-sector partnership. Declared a Time Warner manager: "The literacy level in this country is a crime, and businesses have an obligation to attempt to make an impact on some of the serious social problems that face us. It's about looking at the national agenda, because none of the other benefits to us are profound enough to justify the expense and investment that we make here."

Balancing Value

Stronger, more enduring alliances exhibit a balanced exchange of value in the Collaboration Value Construct. As CARE's Phil Johnston observed: "It doesn't work very well and is not sustainable over time when there is an imbalance either way." Benefits seem to flow in both directions and be deemed acceptably commensurate in value when each partner actively seeks ways to advance the other's agenda and each has learned deeply about the other's business. A resource exchange that gets significantly out of balance can erode the dominant benefit provider's motivation to continue investing in the relationship or tempt that provider to exercise undue influence over the recipient partner.[11] John Sawhill finds that TNC and Georgia-Pacific still struggle to break out and stay out of typical partnership roles: "There is a tendency for both the business and the charity to slip backward into traditional roles, where the charity is the seeker and the business is the giver. You have to struggle to keep it as a partnership."

Imbalances can occur because, as happened with CARE and Starbucks, the circumstances of the partners change. At the start of their alliance in 1989, Starbucks was small and CARE big. By 1999, Starbucks had grown enormously, dwarfing CARE, and as a CARE manager observed, it was developing "more layers of people, more bureaucracy. It's growing so fast that it's hard for the people in Starbucks to even know about the CARE partnership." Moreover, Starbucks created its own foundation and launched several initiatives in the United States, so that CARE now finds itself competing with other good causes and nonprofits for the company's attention and resources. "Even though we're still a big beneficiary of Starbucks' generosity," lamented the CARE manager, "we're one of many now. So it's harder for us to find ways to make a mutually beneficial partnership, because there's just a lot more competition internally."

Partners need to continually review the value exchange with one another to ensure that they both perceive the benefit flow to be mutually beneficial and equitably balanced.

Renewing Value

As a collaboration evolves, the value of the benefits can erode. Skills acquired by one partner from another, for example, may no longer be a transferable benefit. Relationships are dynamic and subject to alteration due to changes in the external environment; partners' needs and priorities can change. Even more subtly, successful collaborations can slide into complacency and cease to search for value opportunities. For all of these reasons the original value generated by an alliance can depreciate, giving rise to the need to *renew the value* of collaborations.

Skills are perhaps foremost among the many benefits that disappear as one organization internalizes another's competencies. Timberland, for example, has developed through its interaction with City Year staff a strong internal ability to mount and manage community service projects, thereby diminishing a benefit contributed by City Year. Similarly, some of the management skills imparted by

Timberland executives have now been absorbed by City Year staff. Starbucks has developed considerable knowledge about development projects, even to the point of managing some itself, and no longer needs to defer passively to CARE's expertise and agenda when choosing projects to support. With Starbucks more interested now in maximizing its impact on the specific communities from which it sources coffee than in tagging on to CARE projects "located somewhere in the country," CARE "is doing some projects that maybe otherwise wouldn't have been selected," a CARE manager said. "Not that they're not needy or deserving, but we're choosing one particular geographic area because Starbucks is interested in it." Such developments create both tensions that must be addressed and opportunities for combining the partners' growing knowledge to generate even more effectively designed projects.

Timberland's Ken Freitas explained the tendency for collaboration resource transfers to often have diminishing returns with a business analogy: "We've got some products in our line that sell every day OK, but if we just relied on those [we would] begin to decay as opposed to growing or thriving. I'm glad we're close with City Year because it allows us to build for the next 'product.'" Continuing to rely on the same collaboration formula risks slow decay.

A competitive implication of depreciating value in a collaboration is revealed in the evolution of the alliance between Ralston Purina and the American Humane Association (AHA). In the beginning the AHA served primarily to link Ralston Purina with its member animal shelters. Once the connection was made however, the company could deal directly with the shelters. With AHA's brokering function no longer needed, the strength of the alliance deteriorated.

At such a juncture the partners can either search for new activities or resource exchanges that might renew the alliance's value or continue the relationship at a lower level. AHA did not deem it necessary to engage in renewal because the fundamental mission of increasing animal placement was continuing, having been effectively transferred to member shelters. AHA instead reduced its role to the collection and analysis of statistics for Ralston Purina.

Ralston Purina subsequently incurred a further challenge when competitors began bidding away the shelters with higher grants than Ralston Purina was offering. As it matures, the alliance marketplace hosts both more partnering opportunities and more competition for prospective partners. When a corporation or nonprofit demonstrates that a competitive advantage accrues to a particular alliance, competitors will soon mimic that alliance. Partnerships based predominantly on financial transfers, in particular, are exposed to capture by competitors offering better terms. Multifaceted relationships that involve volunteers, services, joint activities and planning, and strong personal relationships (that is, advanced transactional or integrative stage relationships) tend to be more insulated from competitor's incursions.

Similar advice holds for nonprofits. Warned a Reading Is Fundamental executive: "There is the danger of the nonprofit being treated like any other vendor. There's the advertising firm and the PR firm and the nonprofit. Our relationship with Visa was absolutely not like that, but it happened to us once before and we quickly extricated ourselves from that situation. We were not there to solve a company's problems for it and be treated the same way a fix-it agency would be treated."

Switching vendors is commonplace when relationships are not deeply embedded and when partners do not continually explore new ways to generate mutual benefits.

Finally, any long-term relationship runs the risk of complacency. Said Blomquist of CARE's relationship with Starbucks: "It's been great, but we haven't given it quite enough attention in the last year or two, and we've got to put some new energy and passion into it." A survey of Starbucks personnel revealed continuing strong commitment to the partnership. The challenge lies in finding new initiatives. And in the case of CARE, doing so efficiently, for Blomquist added a constraint: "In the next phase we have to find new ways to produce good things for CARE and for Starbucks, but without requiring huge management and operational time." Absent continuing, value-adding innovations, alliances risk stagnation. Innovation is the antidote to complacency and stagnation.

The imperative of value renewal places a premium on the creative capacity for innovation. In the alliance marketplace, as in the commercial marketplace, failure to innovate and create new value will likely lead to displacement. The entrepreneurial spirit at both Bayer and Bidwell has been a driving force in generating ideas and sustaining the partnership. Both organizations' executives tout entrepreneurship. Bayer's culture and corporate philosophy encourage and sustain individual innovation. "This is not a top-down thing," emphasized a Bayer executive. "It isn't that the corporation strategically planned all these things. What happened is that individuals took initiative in an environment in which the company empowers employees to do the right things and they are inspired by [Bidwell]." Added Benzing: "It's not a bureaucracy. It starts with an individual or several individuals seeing an opportunity, acting on it, and bringing it up to their superiors. The company philosophy encourages that kind of thing. The vice presidents and the people in power say, 'Yeah, we want to support this.' And it gives those people who are directly involved the freedom and satisfaction of doing something that is also supported by their superiors."

Bidwell has also created an environment that fosters innovation. "What I have come to understand is the chemical reaction," explained Strickland. "I understand how to put the ingredients together in such a way that it produces this kind of reaction. My whole theory of management is, if you get enough bright people in one place and you let them be bright, they will be. You don't need the bureaucracy and task forces and study groups. If you keep things focused, people will want to work with you."

Declining value also can lead to a strategic decision to exit an alliance. Collaborations are not necessarily permanent. Value depreciation may not be rectifiable. The circumstances of one partner might change significantly, altering its needs and the value proposition of the alliance; the partners might have seen from the outset that the alliance would last only a specified time or until specific objectives were achieved. Whatever the reason for choosing this course, strategic collaborations represent important institutional assets that are developed through significant investments of time and resources, and decisions to abandon them should be accompanied and supported by the same careful analysis that characterized their creation.

If exit seems desirable, the partner wishing to end the alliance should present the reasons to the other partner to see if any new value-generating ideas that might revitalize the collaboration are forthcoming. If not, the relationship should be dissolved in a manner that minimizes disruption to both the partners and the flow of social benefits. A phase-out period is usually preferable to an abrupt termination. The exiting partner might also offer assistance in finding a replacement partner if that seems desirable. An organization's reputation and desirability as a partner to other organizations can be significantly affected by the way it exits an existing relationship.

Conclusion

Strategic collaborations exist to generate significant value for the partners. The Collaboration Value Construct provides a framework for systematically analyzing the four critical dimensions of value generation in an alliance. Managers from both organizations first need to define the value to be generated and jointly set clear value expectations. When quantitative metrics prove elusive, qualitative assessments may have to be used. Benefits must be weighed against the costs of resources to be deployed in the collaboration and against risks, including the risk to one's reputation.

The second focus of the Collaboration Value Construct analysis is value creation. The magnitude of the value created generally increases as a relationship moves from generic resource transfer to core competencies exchange to joint value creation. The source of value becomes increasingly proprietary and specific to the particular combination of resources marshaled in the alliance. The often quite different and more complex value configurations generated by multiparty collaborations can produce benefits to society well beyond the strengthening of an NPO; the combined resources of corporate and nonprofit partners can generate additional social value that would not exist in the absence of the collaboration.

The third element of the Collaboration Value Construct analysis is value balance, the requirements that the resource flow be two-way and of commensurate worth to both partners. A partner that perceives that it is giving much more than it is getting may well stop investing in a relationship or begin to exercise undue influence over the other partner. This balancing act requires continual concentration and effort.

The final element of the Collaboration Value Construct analysis is value renewal. Collaboration benefits can depreciate over time as a consequence of changing partner circumstances and needs or the internalization of partners' transferred competencies. This gives rise to the imperative of continual innovation and entrepreneurial creation of new value-adding collaborative activities. The capacity for renewal is part of the organizational learning that occurs in vibrant alliances. A partner that ceases to innovate and generate distinctive value is likely to be displaced by a more aggressive or creative competitor. This risk of displacement is greater when the relationship is at a lower level on the Collaboration Continuum. More developed, complex, and dynamic relationships in the advanced transactional or integrative stages impose more barriers to entry by competitors. When renewal is neither possible nor desirable, then termination is the appropriate strategic choice, but care should be taken to exit constructively, lest one's reputation as a desirable partner be blemished.

6

Managing the Relationship

We saw in the last chapter that the sustainability of a strategic alliance rests fundamentally on the continued generation of value to the partners. The ultimate effectiveness of an alliance, however, is a function of how well the partners manage their interaction. It is important that a partnership be viewed as a relationship rather than a deal. Like any valued relationship, a collaborative alliance prospers to the degree that the partners invest in it.

The key areas of concern in relationship management are organization, trust, communication, accountability, and learning. In order to be strong, alliances need to be organized to capture the focused attention of the leadership; systems and procedures can then be developed so that the partnership transcends that leadership. The strength of a relationship also depends on the depth of trust that can be cultivated between the partners. In addition, relationships are developed through effective communication between the partners and through equally necessary communication within each organization and between the organizations and their outside stakeholders. Moreover, strategic partners hold high expectations of one another and demand accountability for meeting them; accountability presumes commitment and the ability to fulfill obligations. Finally, cross-sector collaboration being exceedingly complex, it is best treated as a continual learning experience.

As the alliance marketplace continues to mature and organizations begin maintaining multiple cross-sector relationships, they will need to actively manage not just single but multiple complex relationships. This chapter closes with a discussion of how to manage a collaboration portfolio.

Organizing the Alliance

An alliance first takes shape in people's minds, and then, as thoughts turn to actions, the processes through which the alliance does its work must gain stability, embedding themselves in institutional procedures.

Focused Attention

Strong alliances have the focused attention of the partners. They must capture sufficient mind share among key leaders and implementers to command and deploy the resources required to achieve impact. Consider, for example, the relationship between City Year and Timberland. Although Timberland contributes to many nonprofit organizations, its energies, resources, and strategy are focused overwhelmingly on its relationship with City Year. The $1 million worth of cash and in-kind support it annually provides to City Year is considerably more than its maximum grants to other organizations of about $10,000, and personnel interaction with other nonprofits is much less frequent and on a much smaller scale than it is with City Year. Rather than spread its attention and resources across many relationships, Timberland has consciously chosen to focus primarily on one strategic alliance.

City Year's partnering portfolio cannot be as exclusive as Timberland's. In fact, Timberland, recognizing the nonprofit's need for more funding to support expansion and engage more businesses in community service, has helped recruit some of the 654 corporate donors and 67 corporate sponsors of City Year's youth corps teams. Nevertheless, during fiscal year 1998, Timberland provided 71 percent of corporate support for City Year's national operations and 18 percent of corporate support for its entire network (private sector sources provide slightly more than half of City Year's total budget, AmeriCorps most of the balance). Timberland was the first corporate partner to take its relationship with City Year to a fuller level of engagement. Viewed as a laboratory for innovation and primary model for partnering, the relationship with Timberland receives the highest allocation of City Year's leadership time.

To ensure adequate attention to a collaborative relationship, each partner should designate a *partner relationship manager,* as a Beginning with Children spokesperson says Pfizer did for that nonprofit: "Pfizer is a huge company, but it is an efficient one. We have always had a contact person who was very effective. Our program has been facilitated because of our relationship with this person." Both Reading Is Fundamental and Visa dedicated staff to the management of their relationship. Without individuals with designated responsibility for the relationship on both sides, communication is likely to be ad hoc, responsibility diluted, and actions uncoordinated. A related approach is to organize alliance responsibilities on a project basis, with the partners developing an agreement that specifies objectives and roles and responsibilities for each new collaboration project according to its unique characteristics.

To define and implement its environmental strategy, Georgia-Pacific has personnel dedicated to the task, including Lee Thomas, who sets strategy, Rob Olszewski, who manages partnerships at the corporate level, and the local area managers, who handle the relationships day-to-day. The Nature Conservancy (TNC) has likewise appointed account managers to its key partnerships. "You need someone on both sides who has overall responsibility," emphasized TNC president John Sawhill. "When we haven't had that in some of our cause-related marketing partnerships, it's made it more difficult because there isn't necessarily anybody on the corporate side thinking about how to move the relationships forward."

"You'd always rather be dealing with someone who is close to the basic business of the company," Sawhill added. "But you can't pick whom you work with, so you end up with the charitable giving arm or environment, health, and safety person. But sometimes that person can be your champion and has a budget [for philanthropic programs, unlike a business unit leader]."

Institutionalization

Although leader involvement is essential to the success of a collaboration, to ensure continuity and broaden impact other people must be engaged and procedures developed. The organizations, not just the leaders, must own the alliance.

Conceived and fostered by top executives, the alliance between City Year and Timberland has gone beyond a top-to-top relationship and is now embedded in the broader organizational structures. The process has not been without difficulty, according to leaders of both organizations, one problem being that no single individual at City Year was responsible for the relationship on a daily basis. Elyse Klysa, who manages Timberland's Social Enterprise Department, has played the account executive role on the Timberland side. Recently City Year designated a person to be her counterpart. Klysa thought that the ad hoc, informal manner in which the relationship was previously managed had impeded institutionalization.

An accompanying challenge is to make the relationship part of both organizations' cultures. One way Timberland maintains a presence at City Year is through supplying the uniforms that City Year staff wear daily. City Year achieves a periodic presence within Timberland primarily by providing staff to assist with on-site training and service projects. Organizations should heed the caution of Timberland vice president of social enterprise Ken Freitas that there is a risk in becoming "too complacent, getting very focused on managing through today versus building for tomorrow," and should not overlook the importance of institutionalizing the processes of shared visioning and value renewal by setting aside explicit times for these activities.

Bidwell founder Bill Strickland and retired Bayer vice president Peter Benzing, under whose leadership the Bidwell-Bayer alliance flourished, acknowledge that the challenge remains to institutionalize that partnership, so that many more individuals across both organizations embrace it. "If I left this relationship, I would want to make sure that somebody [at Bayer] would be interested in carrying on the legacy," insisted Benzing. I don't think you work this hard at establishing good partnerships and not want them to continue. You have to pass the torch; it's a people-oriented thing." According to some Bayer executives, few employees beyond those directly involved with Bidwell are aware of the relationship. "I would say it falls into the category of, 'Oh, I've heard of that,'" observed Bayer Foundation executive director Sande Deitch. Although the alliance has migrated toward the integrative stage on the Collaboration Continuum, its relationship network must be significantly broadened if it is to achieve deeper organizational integration. Benzing, identified by Bidwell and Bayer executives alike as the core of the relationship, contended that "enough other people in the corporation have taken a significant interest and are actively supporting Bidwell that, if I drop dead today, this will continue. I don't think there's any question about it."

One way to institutionalize alliance leadership is by creating joint management structures. The land management team established by Georgia-Pacific and The Nature Conservancy under the Roanoke agreement (as described in Chapter Four) comprised representatives of both organizations and nonvoting members of state and federal environmental agencies. This team, which spent a substantial amount of time meeting to "hammer out the details," according to Sawhill, will be responsible for ongoing management of the land. This type of management structure helped to build consensus on the terms of the ecosystem management plan and will ensure that decisions moving forward are made by the partners together and in accordance with the original intent of the agreement. "You can't specify everything on land management," Olszewski pointed out. "You learn and decide as you progress, so the on-the-ground relationships are very important." To help finance the ongoing costs of local management in the Roanoke, Georgia-Pacific conveyed hunting rights to TNC, which in turn could sell licenses to hunters.

Georgia-Pacific senior communications manager Lynn Klein emphasized the challenge of maintaining the original intent of an agreement given the long-term nature of projects and short-term nature of job assignments. "I think the toughest part," she said, "is trying to be true to the original agreement given personnel changes. The foresters who were involved in the original agreement can get transferred somewhere, and The Nature Conservancy has had some personnel changes, too." Documenting agreements and making multiple individuals responsible for them provides some hedge against disruptions caused by personnel turnover.

"Once the proposal is put together we put together a team," explained an MCI/WorldCom executive. "It's not one person, like a project manager. Their Web site people are hooked up with our Web site people, their PR people with our PR people, their marketing people with ours. It's truly a partnership. That team then puts together the implementation plan and time frame." The National Geographic Society's spokesperson concurred: "On multiple occasions MCI WorldCom has gotten all the partners together. Every step of the way they've been very inclusive."

Institutionalizing a shift to a cooperative relationship requires incentives that motivate a change in individual behavior. Both Georgia-Pacific and TNC have developed incentive systems that reward collaborative behavior. Georgia-Pacific ties a small part of individuals' bonuses to their performance on the eleven-point Forest Resources Environmental Strategy, but "the stronger influence on them is peer pressure," according to Olszewski. "It's stronger than the bonus plan. We'll occasionally bring them together and they'll do presentations on their eleven-point strategy. And if one of them is lagging way far behind, you'd be surprised how that works. They see that their peers are doing it. They're getting complimented for it. It looks like the right thing to do, and that makes them think differently."

On the importance of incorporating partnership activities into performance objectives, Sawhill added: "Establish someone in the corporation who has a clear responsibility for making the partnership work—someone who says, 'This is my job. This is in my annual objectives. I've got to get this done.' What gets measured is what gets done."

Building Trust

Trust is the essential intangible asset of effective alliances, the interpersonal webbing that knits organizations together and facilitates concerted action. Communication and interaction are central to the trust-building process. The Beginning with Children executive observed that "you have to build respect in the entity you're trying to help, and you can't do that by sending a newsletter or giving a call every year or giving a party or taking people out to dinner once a year. It's really all in the attitude." Added a Reebok manager, "I think a lot of time is spent on 'what the deal is,' but people don't do enough matching up of corporate cultures. You need to make the effort to really understand each other, to talk about more than just the legal document on the table." "It's not like a grant and that's the end of it," emphasized an executive from Merck. "Partnerships, to be successful, have to have the continuing involvement of both partners."

"We shared visions and goals for what we would like to accomplish together up front," explained a National Science Resources Center (NSRC) manager, "This led to the establishment of mutual goals and a sense of trust. From there, the floodgates of communication opened. We have no problem saying, 'That's a half-cocked idea.' We listen to each other. I talk to our partners at least once a month, some weekly." A staff member of Reading Is Fundamental described how "the people at Visa and their advertising firm were very open to our ideas and our way of thinking, which was sometimes very different from what they were thinking. It worked because we built a level of trust. And that can't be theoretical. That has to be based on people and the way people work: meeting deadlines and being honest with each other. When we felt that some messages were not appropriate, we let them know and they would understand."

The more personal the relationship glue, the stronger an alliance's cohesion, and this cohesion is central to the institutionalization process. Joint activities such as service projects, training sessions, and mutual technical assistance created opportunities for developing new relationships within the City Year–Timberland alliance. An entire generation of staff and corps members were trained at City Year by working at some level on the Timberland relationship, and hundreds of Timberland employees have interacted with City Year staff. Timberland COO Jeff Swartz explained that "by putting ordinary people together in an ordinary context you create common experience. One of our marketing people who provided some assistance to City Year came back and said, 'It had been clear to me how Timberland does service with City Year and saves the world. It had been less clear to me how Timberland does its job day-to-day and saves the world. I went and did my job today and I saved the world.'"

"We've informed their culture the same way they've informed ours," added Freitas. "There is a different view [at City Year] of what business can be and what role business can play."

"As we explore corporate relationships," explained CARE president Peter Bell, "we feel most comfortable where first there is a relationship between senior executives at CARE and our corporate counterparts. It has to be more than a public relations or a charity relationship. It has to be more fulsome than that. The financial aspects are important, but they do not make the relationship. There has to be sufficient mutual respect and trust so that we can talk about problems and issues in an open and frank way."

Starbucks senior vice president Dave Olsen observed in the Starbucks-CARE alliance a "deep appreciation by each of what the other does in the course of its regular business," and a CARE manager remarked that the relationship "evolved because of the human dynamic of a few people getting together who really like one another, have respect for each other, and share a common vision and goal." Reflecting on the many misconceptions that nonprofits and corporations tend to have about one another, a CARE manager remarked that "you have to sit down and talk with each other and develop trust, and that takes time. It starts with one or two individuals and works down. You've got to filter that learning and trust through the organization. You have to be aware of your own and your partner's cultures."

Relationships at the top of partner organizations are necessary but not sufficient to sustain and grow a partnership. The more points of connection, the stronger the relationship. Georgia-Pacific's Lynn Klein emphasized the importance of "making sure that everybody's comfortable from the executive level down to the actual forester who's going to interface day-to-day with The Nature Conservancy person who's charged with managing that area. The executives and PR people can come in and out and talk about it, but then you have to make sure that the foresters and The Nature Conservancy people at the local level are okay with the partnership and okay talking with each other."

Added Rob Olszewski: "If the local leaders have not bought in and it gets forced down and they're not happy about that, they have the potential of throwing a cog in there."

Georgia-Pacific group manager Alex Hopkins echoed these sentiments. "The interpersonal relationships built in these types of partnerships are critical," he insisted. "I can't overemphasize their importance. It's easy to identify a group or a company as your adversary if you don't have a personal interaction with that group." "One of the reasons that the Roanoke agreement emerged," Olszewski stated, "was a combination of the personalities. Al Hopkins, who was our group manager out of the Raleigh area, took a significant personal interest in this whole endeavor, probably more aggressively than some of our other guys did at the time. And that was important. He struck up a pretty good relationship with folks from TNC in Chapel Hill."

"In a big, multinational corporation a multiple approach works best," maintained Sawhill. "We build strong relationships with the people in the communities where we're working and we also build a relationship at the top of the corporation so that when I call the CEO he answers the telephone. Georgia-Pacific is a good example. The people in these different project areas have good strong relationships. And we've got [Georgia-Pacific CEO] Pete [Correll] on our board so the people down the line know that there is good support at the top. You really need both in order to succeed. We have failed at times when we've had one and not the other."

Sawhill also stressed the importance of being able to engage individual employees in the partnership. "We have lots of volunteer opportunities and ways that individuals can give out of their paycheck and specify where the money goes (for example, to the state where they grew up)," he explained. "So there's really a way to build some sense of corporate pride and momentum." And Olszewski commented: "This relationship continues to grow. There's a lot of probing and restructuring and thinking that we do and that TNC folks do that makes it grow and modify over time, which is good." Each project opens the door for more personal connections, mutual understanding, and trust development, and with each success the collaboration develops more confidence to attempt increasingly complex and important initiatives. The Altamaha project, for example, would not even have hit the radar screen had it not been for the success of the Roanoke agreement. Olszewski emphasized the importance of such incremental evolutionary processes: "Let the relationship grow over time. Don't try to leap from level one to level ten; all those levels in between are important, because you develop mutual organizational trust."

A number of alliances surveyed had a higher degree of relational complexity through the involvement of multiple levels and parties. Also involved in the alliance between Pfizer and Beginning with Children is the local board of education; the collaboration between Hewlett-Packard and the National Science Resources Center includes school district administrators and teachers; MCI World-Com's alliance to encourage Internet-based learning embraces six nonprofits and school districts and teachers across the country; and Time Warner's partnership with Time to Read engages a different nonprofit organization and a different part of the company in each city in which the program operates. Managing multiple relationships effectively, albeit challenging, can significantly magnify an alliance's impact. This broader result is precisely what The Nature Conservancy and Georgia-Pacific are striving to achieve by enlisting the support of additional companies and governmental agencies in their Altamaha project.

Communicating Effectively

Partners must work to develop ongoing and effective communication between themselves, among the personnel within each organization, and with outside stakeholders and others about the alliance's mission, activities, needs, and accomplishments.

Between the Partners

Communication being central to building trust and managing the collaboration process, City Year and Timberland were initially challenged to overcome their respective gratefulness and charity syndromes, which tended to preclude all but the most perfunctory communication between them. It was only when City Year's top executives actively engaged Timberland's that the two sides began to discover the possible benefits of greater collaboration. The gold was not discovered until they started digging.

The communication challenge is perennially present. City Year cofounder Michael Brown has described *"The Gift of the Magi" problem,* for example, which arises when one side tries to do something positive for the other without ascertaining if the other attaches a similar value to it. For example, Timberland put a lot of effort into planning a concert to embellish City Year's annual Serve-a-thon only to have City Year leaders, when they realized that it was not feasible given the nonprofit's capabilities and the other demands of the Serve-a-thon, regretfully decline this gift. "After that experience," recalled Brown, "we made a decision that we would never try to surprise each other with things, that we would really try to involve each other early on, from the very beginning, and be very honest, [that we would ask] 'Are you interested in this? If so, under what time frame, under what conditions?'"

Among other forces that complicate communication are crises and other stressful periods during which communication with the alliance partners is often crowded out. "The urgent isn't necessarily the important," observed City Year cofounder Alan Khazei, "but that's what gets the attention. Our relationship has gotten weaker when we haven't had those regular communications." He added that one of the greatest current difficulties is scheduling meetings between the organizations' leaders. As both City Year and Timberland have grown tremendously over the past ten years, time demands on the executives have increased and their schedules have become more complicated. Swartz's chairmanship of the City Year board ensures periodic meetings, and City Year leaders continue to find time to make presentations to Timberland employees during key company events such as sales meetings.

Communication between partners becomes particularly critical when difficulties arise, as Ralston Purina has learned. "A number of years ago we tried to make a change in the Pets for People program and it was a misstep. It was a huge error," recalled a company manager. "What I did in order to get us back on track with our shelter partners was invite a key group of shelter directors in. The most important thing is to keep in constant communication with them, know what works for them. Know what they're doing. Know what makes sense. Tell them what you're thinking about doing before you do it."

Within Each Organization

Internal communication is also important. A Reebok executive, for example, described how that company "had a huge campaign to make sure that people read about this partnership [with Amnesty International], not just in the annual report. There were constantly stories in the employee newsletter and ways to get involved. The extent to which you make things accessible to employees increases knowledge and pride." An executive from the American Humane Association recommended that partners "be very verbal about the cause. Share it widely with the employees, and help it permeate the culture so that the employees feel that by doing their job they are helping to achieve some good. That is really extending the arms of a partnership. This is especially true if it is a second- or third- or fourth-generation relationship, as the history of the partnership can get somewhat lost." Visibility reinforces a relationship. Timberland has, according to City Year's Khazei, "more community service iconography around its headquarters than even we do."

To Outsiders

Part of the relationship-building process is publicizing the partnership and crediting the partner. "Because we came out of the private sector to begin with, we are conscious of acknowledging the generosity of the private sector," emphasized a Beginning with Children manager. United Way of Seattle ensures that signs and literature recognizing Nordstrom's generosity are prominently displayed. Additionally, according to this nonprofit's manager, "We had an event to provide recognition to a new program, and we held that event at Nordstrom." Corporations, like nonprofits, value visibility. Advised the Jimmy Fund's spokesperson, "Never underestimate how much the corporations seek recognition. It is better to fault on the side of too much than not enough." Corporations themselves often err in this direction, according to Starbucks's Olsen. "You're at risk of sounding too boastful if you beat your drum too loudly," he explained, adding: "I believe now that we fell way short of how aggressively we should have talked about this partnership [with CARE]." Similarly, CARE regional director Peter Blomquist indicated that "CARE fell short of giving Starbucks the credit and visibility that was its due." Timberland's Jeff Swartz makes a progress report on community service an integral part of his quarterly report on business results to stockholders and company analysts.

Ensuring Accountability

Partners must have similar expectations about the alliance, have confidence that each partner will follow through, and be able to measure and report their alliance results.

Mutual Expectations

Powerful alliances are built on high mutual expectations. According to Ken Freitas: "The level of expectation is a fundamental part of [the Timberland–City Year] relationship." And Jeff Swartz similarly commented: "The organization that you chose to partner with needs to have the same commitment to powerful notions and the same ability to deliver on these as you do. If they are not at the same level, the equation falls apart and the relationship doesn't work."

Relationships in the philanthropic stage tend to be characterized by relatively low expectations. Giving is viewed as the end point in the transaction, and because it is assumed that the funds will be put to good use by the beneficiary NPO, little time is invested in delineating performance expectations and even less in ascertaining ultimate results. As partners migrate further along the Collaboration Continuum, however, the perspective begins to shift from *giving* to *investing* and from *one-way* to *two-way* performance expectations.

Surveyed partners emphasized the importance of being very clear about what each partner is seeking and about defining the deliverables. High expectations generate high performance standards, which promote value creation and foster mutual accountability, which in turn motivate execution responsibility.

Commitment and Execution

Mutual expectations are translated into results through commitment and execution capability. An extended time horizon is implicit in serious commitment. Starbucks' Dave Olsen recounts a conversation with two senior CARE staff in Ethiopia, in which he said: "It's okay if we don't have flashy results and big stories to tell and pictures to show at the end of a year. We recognize this stuff takes longer." His listeners' jaws dropped in amazement because they had never heard a donor say this before.

A similar intent was expressed by a Hewlett-Packard executive: "We want to be there for the long term. We want to involve our employees as volunteers. We want to add value." "For many corporations, the first interest is the local community," observed the spokesperson from the National Science Resources Center, Hewlett-Packard's partner. "It takes a huge amount of work to get a private sector organization to invest in a national institution. The incentive for them to partner with us is that we had a well thought out business plan. They realized that their involvement with us could show results at the local level for us and for them. Now we are moving on to urban districts where HP does not have a local presence. The company is moving beyond their own communities to work on the education agenda, which is amazing."

The College Fund (UNCF) also defined commitment in terms of willingness to take on major challenges. "When you're talking about major initiatives that will create some sustainable change in the country," explained a UNCF manager, "what's really important is that you have a comprehensive outlook on what needs to be done. You can't just take bits and pieces; you have to take the whole ball of wax. And you have to do it over a long period of time. Not all corporations are willing to do that. Merck stepped up and said, 'What do we need to do, and how can we measure it at the end?' Merck is a company that has the tenacity to do a program [of science internships] like this. We have received absolutely fantastic results."

"I view it like advertising," observed the spokesperson for the American Humane Association. "There are ways that you can portray your company and you need to invest in what people know about you. Oftentimes it takes a multiyear commitment until consumers get to know you in a certain way. A short-term project doesn't do that."

As relationships move further along the Collaboration Continuum, the scale and complexity of engagement expand, intensifying the demands on the partners to execute their commitments effectively. "We provide an opportunity for massive engagement, and that's fraught with difficulty and challenge," observed City Year's Michael Brown. "Even if 90 percent of this ongoing stream of engagements are great, there's 10 percent that aren't. The potential is huge, but on the downside it's a lot of execution. And in our heavily idea-driven environment, the constant iteration of new ideas burdens the ongoing execution lines." The capability to meet expanding commitments being critical to partners' ongoing credibility, balancing demands with execution capability is an ever-present challenge, albeit one that can be met jointly. And with such organizational capabilities being enhanced by personnel training and systems development, joint investment in such activities is well advised. Too often funders of NPOs, trying to direct as much money as possible into service delivery that targets beneficiaries, cut back too far on the amount of money channeled into organizational development. The perverse effect is that the NPOs' organizational capabilities remain underdeveloped and their effectiveness is hindered.[1] Businesses continually invest in their own administrative capacity in order to improve performance; they should do the same for their NPO partners.

Performance Accountability

Accountability accompanies high expectations as a critical part of the relationship management process. "Individuals in charge of corporate giving are becoming more accountable for what they give," observed the UNCF's spokesperson. "While they understand the necessity for unrestricted grants, the primary way for them to account for what they give is through restricted funding, where they are better able to measure outcomes." Partners must be able to demonstrate to what extent they have produced expected benefits.

A National Science Resources Center manager remarked, for example, "We have quality products and services that we have to demonstrate are effective. The corporations like the quality assurance standards that we maintain. We research and evaluate everything we do. Every program has a 5 percent to 10 percent part of the budget that is dedicated to that." The MCI WorldCom executive surveyed indicated that it applies its best practices to measurement: "Our measurement is very quantitative. We probably have more scientifically measured results than many foundations."

Performance assessment of social purpose collaborations is complicated by the difficulty of measuring many types of social betterment outcomes. The impact of programs aimed, for example, at attitudinal or behavioral change or quality-of-life improvements might not be manifested until much later and can be difficult to measure with precision. Moreover, attribution of a result to the intervention might be confounded by other factors that exerted an influence on the outcomes. Businesses that employ the straightforward calculation of a financial return on investment are often frustrated by less precise methods of assessing the return on their social investment. Because the diversity of programs and outcomes complicates the development of a standard methodology, partners discussing the benefits and additional social impact they expect the alliance to generate should articulate how these elements are to be measured as well as achieved. Then they can individually devise performance indicators to assess their respective benefits and can jointly establish quantitative and qualitative measures of the social value generated by their combined efforts.

Beyond these indicators, it is useful for partners to meet regularly to inquire whether each partner's expectations are being met. Such *accountability checkups* can identify expectation gaps. The process should entail a discussion of what each partner might do to further strengthen the alliance. Useful questions include: What should I do better? What should I be doing that I am not doing? How can we work together in different ways to be even more effective?

Accountability is more than living up to commitments; it encompasses a continual search for improvement.

Pursuing Learning

The partnering process should be a learning process; the partners must discover how to manage a relationship and its benefits and must garner the particular expertise the relationship demands for its success.

Partnering Process

Many organizations view their strategic partnerships as *alliance learning laboratories*. Because strategic cross-sector collaboration differs fundamentally from other types of partnering and because organizations have relatively less experience with such relationships, partners must learn by doing. This means they must recognize that no one has all the answers, and they must be open to mutual exploration and discovery and be willing to experiment.

"Our people are land deal makers and our scientists like to control the land," explained TNC's Sawhill, "So our G-P relationship is teaching us how to partner, and it is enabling us to develop cooperative relationships with other forest products companies." Georgia-Pacific senior vice president John Rasor agrees: "One of the big benefits of this relationship is that it is teaching us about partnering."

Georgia-Pacific and TNC have made progress in overcoming old perceptions, and the change in attitude has been noticeable. Olszewski has observed an improvement in Georgia-Pacific's comfort level in dealing with nonprofit organizations, a change he says is most in evidence at the senior executive level. As they have developed a better understanding of one another, the two organizations have become more receptive to new ideas. "Just being open to the idea of meeting and listening and talking to people and not necessarily assuming that you can't do anything together—that's been a big lesson learned for all of us," commented Lynn Klein. "There's been an impact on the culture. We do a lot more sitting down at the table and talking through things up front." Success in new kinds of partnerships has also opened minds; had Georgia-Pacific not entered into the agreement on the Lower Roanoke River, explained Klein, it might not have considered doing anything differently in its agreement with the state of Florida.

City Year and Timberland also consider their relationship to be a learning laboratory. As Ken Freitas succinctly stated, "It is not formulaic." Because there is no standard formula, there is continued willingness on both sides to explore and try out new activities and relationship dimensions. The partners seem to share a discovery ethic that fosters striving for an ever-deeper and richer relationship. Inherent in the organizations' visioning now is a longer time perspective, all the more powerful because it reduces the risk that short-term operating problems might derail the relationship.

Expertise Development

In the stronger alliances there was recognition of the need to develop new capabilities for managing the collaboration more effectively. Olszewski and his staff across the country, for example, provide support and guidance to Georgia-Pacific's profit center managers as they seek appropriate partners and try to develop innovative plans. Additionally, the corporate legal and tax departments are available to put together agreements, and the communications department is willing to develop fact sheets and help determine the best way to announce a joint project, maximizing its public relations value.

TNC also faced the challenge of developing new organizational capabilities. "We created a cause-related marketing program," Sawhill recounted. "Prior to 1990, there really was no cause-related marketing program in the country. And now it's a predominant form of corporate philanthropy, and that transition happened overnight. So we basically had to start a program from scratch and get some expertise in it real fast. Organizational flexibility is really critical. You have to attract new skills to your organization to respond to these opportunities. The corporate sector is moving very fast these days, and we have to keep up with that."

As vibrant collaborations grow so does the partners' capacity to identify new opportunities for creating value. As partners learn more about each other's competencies and about the nature of the social problem being addressed, they are better able to envision new ways of combining their resources and working together to capture synergies. This ability to learn and innovate is essential to value renewal.

The Collaboration Portfolio

The points discussed in this chapter are vital to managing any single cross-sector relationship. Most nonprofits and corporations, however, are involved in multiple collaborative relationships, often accumulated more or less ad hoc. To manage multiple relationships strategically, it is useful to think of them as a *collaboration portfolio*.

Taking the Collaboration Inventory

The initial step in analyzing a collaboration portfolio is to make an inventory of existing relationships. This inventory may be elaborated by answering the following questions.

What types of collaborations are we involved in? Categorize alliances by type: first, by the organizations involved (that is, NPO-NPO, NPO-government, NPO-foundation, and NPO-corporation) and, second, by their location on the Collaboration Continuum (that is, philanthropic, transactional, integrative, or a hybrid of these stages). This effectively creates a *collaboration map* that clarifies where the organization currently is with its relationships, which is prerequisite to figuring out where it wants to be.

What are the purposes of our collaborations? Delineate the primary purpose of each alliance category and each alliance. Again, referring back to typical alliance characteristics by stage on the Collaboration Continuum (Table 2.1) can clarify the roles that various collaborations are playing. Collaborations being strategic vehicles, understanding their functions is essential to determining their most effective use.

How important are our collaborations? Rank the importance of each collaboration category and the specific alliances within each category in terms of relative contribution to the organization's larger strategy and mission. Strategy formulation involves allocating scarce resources and choosing among options; prioritizing collaborations is an intrinsic part of that process.

Managing the Portfolio

There are two basic strategic issues to consider in shaping and managing the collaboration portfolio: *mix* and *size*. Each NPO and corporation will have a unique preferred configuration of these two issues, because the task involves creating a portfolio that fits each organization's particular circumstances.

The primary criteria to use in making the mix decision are *balance* and *focus*. As the different types and purposes of collaboration identified in the inventory may all be important to accomplishing an organization's mission, the task will be to determine how much emphasis to place on each collaboration based on its relative contribution. For example, a nonprofit might see from its collaboration inventory that the bulk of its corporate relationships are in the philanthropic stage and that their primary function is fundraising. The nonprofit might then judge that it could mobilize even greater financial and nonfinancial resources by moving a segment of these partners into the transactional stage. It might further deem that considerable strategic advantage could accrue from migrating some relationships all the way to the integrative stage. To develop such relationships, however, will require significant managerial time and effort. Accordingly, the NPO decides to restrict that effort to a single alliance. Thus, it creates a portfolio mix balanced by type and function that, first, retains a large number of traditional philanthropic relationships that generate a dependable revenue base in a cost-effective manner; second, adds a new segment of higher-yielding partners that will provide new streams of revenue (perhaps through cause-related marketing) or new inflows of particular expertise; and third, targets a special effort at developing a deep, high-payoff relationship with a single strategic partner.

The mix of a collaboration portfolio can also depend on the focus of a corporation's social engagement strategy. To try to do everything would be as nonsensical in the social arena as in the marketplace. Priorities should be set, resources focused, and synergies captured. A company should delineate social need areas that are important to its communities and customers and fit its interests and competencies. Citibank, for example, shifted from a community activities policy of "let a thousand flowers bloom" to a focus on two key areas. "Before," recounted one executive, "Citibank was involved in everything from cleaning up beaches to orphanages to programs for disabled people, all of which are nice and useful things to do, but left us with no identity as a company for what we're doing in the community." The subsequent "embedded bank" strategy, designed to show Citibank as a strong and valuable contributor to the economy in its markets and a local problem solver, afforded the "opportunity for us to get some 'branding' for our community programs."

Citibank launched two initiatives. The first was Banking on Enterprise, a $10 million, five-year effort to fund not-for-profit organizations operating microenterprise lending programs in Citibank markets across the globe. In addition to grants, the corporation has used its banking expertise to devise innovative financial instruments and services to support this underserved segment of the financial markets. When creating focus for community engagement activities and enhancing social impact, examine the competencies required for each proposed focus and ensure that they are corporate core competencies. As the Citibank executive put it: "Why would you take on something about which you have no expertise internally? In order not to marginalize our activities in the community, they need to be an extension of who we are as a business." Citibank created several strategic alliances to implement this effort—for example, with ACCION International, a leading microenterprise promoter for which Citibank had been the banker for many years. ACCION helped Citibank learn about the microenterprise field, and Citibank's name enhanced the credibility of the microfinance movement through these partnership arrangements.

The second initiative, Banking on Education, is a $25 million, decade-long effort begun in 1990 to strengthen public education. This effort has involved partnering with urban schools, training teachers, supplying new classroom technologies, and providing Citibank employees to partner NPOs as mentors, tutors, and board members. Citigroup chairman and co-chief John S. Reed has stated that the company "should have an organized approach in every country and make a conscious decision about what we do and how much we do," and most of Citibank's donations now go to education and community development rather than being spread thinly across many areas. As a result of this more focused and prioritized strategy, Citibank's portfolio of alliances has changed dramatically in terms of the types and numbers of NPOs with which the company collaborates.

For any given portfolio mix an organization must also decide on the number of alliances to undertake. This will be largely determined by the partner's capacity to manage its collaboration commitments competently. Timberland's strategy, for example (consistent with its approach to its commercial suppliers, which is to develop a strategic relationship with one or a few suppliers), has been to concentrate its community partnering on its alliance with City Year. Explained COO Swartz: "Why should you triple source a part if you could spend the same amount of time to really get it right with one organization? We had to develop an intimacy to get it right. I couldn't imagine doing this kind of thing with more than one organization." Although Timberland contributes to a number of nonprofit organizations and engages in community service projects with others, the level of these involvements pales in comparison to the involvement with City Year.

Conclusion

Partnerships require a continual investment of time and energy. How an alliance is managed ultimately determines its effectiveness. The focused attention of leaders and implementers, important in its own right, is reinforced by designating partner relationship managers with assigned responsibilities. Sustainability is achieved by institutionalizing the alliance, by diffusing involvement and management responsibility throughout the partner organizations. Incentive systems should reward collaboration with the partner so this ethic can become embedded in the organizational cultures. Strong relationships developed at all levels in the organization over time foster trust, which enables organizations to become better problem solvers and assume greater risks.

Communication between partners needs to be frequent, meaningful, frank, and constructive. Explicit strategies should exist for communicating both internally within the organizations and externally in order to promote and increase the visibility of the alliance.

High mutual expectations motivate superior performance. Accountability for realizing their respective commitments presupposes deep commitments on the part of the partners, characterized by longer time horizons and the willingness to tackle significant problems. Underlying the alliance management process is ongoing learning about how to partner more effectively and create greater value.

Strategic management of multiple alliances can be facilitated by thinking in terms of a collaboration portfolio. A first step in developing such a portfolio is to inventory existing collaborations in terms of type, purpose, and relative importance. The shaping and the management of the portfolio seek to achieve a mix of alliances that effectively contribute to the organization's strategy and mission. Care must also be exercised in determining the size of the portfolio in terms of the number and complexity of alliances relative to the organization's capacity to manage them. One key guideline on portfolio size is clear: overcommitting and underperforming is a sure way to cause partner disillusionment and disengagement.

Collaboration Drivers and Enablers
Jumpstart and American Eagle Outfitters

I n the previous chapters I drew on the experiences of many different partners to illustrate and analyze key processes in the design and operation of collaborative alliances. This chapter provides an integrative view of cross-sector collaboration in a single strategic alliance. The evolutionary dynamics of the alliance are examined, and the key drivers, enablers, and challenges of collaboration are viewed as an integrated whole.

Relationship Overview

Jumpstart, a new, Boston-based NPO founded in 1994 to prepare low-income preschoolers to enter kindergarten ready to succeed, brings children and their parents together with college students as tutors. The college students are recruited through Jumpstart's partnership with AmeriCorps, the national service corps, which provides living stipends and educational scholarships to participating members. Jumpstart has enjoyed strategic partnerships with various organizations, both nonprofit and for-profit, to support and promote its

My thanks to Harvard Business School research associate Arthur McCaffrey, who played a primary role in preparing the initial version of the case study in this chapter.

service goals and activities. Recently, it partnered with Pittsburgh-headquartered American Eagle Outfitters (AEO), which markets a line of clothing for young adults. Notwithstanding their other collaborations, past and present, these two organizations are now embarked together on a new kind of venture in terms of scope and level of commitment.

Begun in 1997, this joint enterprise resulted from an accidental encounter and a modest donation of T-shirts. "We started with Jumpstart in a really small way," recalled American Eagle Outfitters CEO George Kolber. "We didn't know where we were going to go with this. We didn't have any long-term strategic plans." Subsequent development was rapid and deep, however, leading Kolber to assert in September 1998, "I don't think that we will be in any such deep a program with anyone else other than Jumpstart, because it just fits our organization."

Evolutionary Dynamics

Cross-sector relationships can evolve along the Collaboration Continuum at quite different paces, and the Jumpstart-AEO alliance is notable for the rapidity with which it accelerated through the philanthropic stage, moved deeply into the transactional stage of resource exchange, and as the partners pursue the opportunity to scale up to a national level, is entering the integrative stage. Of particular interest are the factors that enabled this alliance to develop so rapidly and richly.

One underlying factor worthy of note is that this alliance built on the experience and knowledge of other cross-sector collaborations. In particular, Jumpstart consciously embraced the City Year–Timberland partnership as a model. Several Jumpstart board members who were closely associated with City Year formed a lateral learning link to that NPO's collaboration experience. Board members often play a critical networking function for their NPOs. This model gave Jumpstart CEO Aaron Lieberman a vision of the possibilities of such alliances and an understanding of some of the elements that contribute to a healthy partnership. The AEO-Jumpstart alliance, by building on others' experiences, was able to be a second-generation alliance, leapfrogging much of its predecessors' time-consuming discovery process. The experience of Jumpstart and AEO will in turn, it is hoped, enable readers to accelerate their own partnership process.

Stage One: Matching Up and Starting Off

As I observed of the more or less happenstance connecting of partners in several of the alliances examined previously, the alliance marketplace is still imperfect. Because information on potential partners and mechanisms for establishing connections are lacking, encounters are often circumstantial. Lieberman emphasized the role of serendipity and luck in bringing him together with Kolber in October 1997.

To obtain exposure, American Eagle Outfitters had helped MTV sponsor a community service award event. Annually, the Do Something Brick Award is given to ten people throughout the country who are under thirty and are making a demonstrable difference in their communities. Lieberman was awarded $10,000 to continue his work with Jumpstart. After the recognition ceremony, he met Kolber, and from there, according to Lieberman, "we moved from the accidental to the strategic." "It wasn't a conscious, preplanned strategy," Kolber added. "It sort of evolved." This encounter between the two CEOs paved the way for leader-led collaboration throughout the following year. Prior experience, stage of development, and distinctive organizational characteristics created an amalgam of attractive features and readiness to partner on both sides. Timing, attitude, preparedness, and personal initiative were key factors in the initiation of Jumpstart's collaboration with AEO. Opportunities are exploited by those prepared to seize them.

If Jumpstart was opportunistic, American Eagle was ripe for the right kind of partner, one that could fulfill a corporate goal of diversity and social engagement that would reflect positively on the company, involve employees in community service, and do some social good. AEO had been involved in other charitable ventures and had donated cash and goods to various worthwhile causes before encountering Jumpstart. Jumpstart crossed its path at a time when it was in the process of reevaluating where to target its social investment "to get the biggest bang for the buck." Explained AEO vice president Susan Miller: "We were giving to anything that came along, which was the easy way out. We did an employee survey that revealed that they were very interested in the company's philanthropic activities, but didn't think that the company was doing a very good job. The nickel-and-diming was killing us. So that really got us going."

Jumpstart's mission of educating underprivileged young children struck a chord at all levels in AEO, particularly with the CEO and the executive committee, who had sponsored the MTV award for Lieberman and had thus done due diligence on his organization. Moreover, observed Kolber, "nobody criticizes education and children. It's not political." A focus on this noncontroversial topic promised to attract wide support in the company. Employees had already demonstrated high interest in community volunteerism through their efforts in an earlier company-sponsored Grand Forks disaster relief project. Jumpstart's mentoring activities held potential for employee volunteer service opportunities. Additionally, Jumpstart's inner-city focus would reinforce AEO's efforts to introduce more diversity into its workforce. Key elements for strategic fit were clearly present.

The partnering process was facilitated by Jumpstart's positive and proactive mind-set toward collaboration. "Our business," emphasized Lieberman, "is helping young children. We're always looking for things that are going to help us do that. Every time we walk through a door, including our own, we say, 'I hope we meet someone who can help us do better today.' That's just part of our attitude and of really trying to be an enterprising and entrepreneurial nonprofit."

Jumpstart was actively seeking to build a relationship very similar to the City Year–Timberland partnership. Lieberman had done his homework and was prepared to make his pitch to anyone who would listen, and AEO was a receptive audience. According to Jumpstart vice president of development Dawn Hutchison, who had corporate partnering experience in a previous nonprofit organization, there was a parallel with other good relationships: "I think that Jumpstart had something very powerful to offer AEO, and they saw that right away. We work with a constituency that they care very much about as consumers, the eighteen- to thirty-five-year-olds [the age group encompassing the AmeriCorps college student volunteers]. And we were also able to bring them access to people and promotional opportunities that they could not get any other place."

A statement in the AEO annual report describing the company's "ideal customer" as someone who "is socially conscious, but practical," in the sense of being concerned about practical ways of improving the world, convinced Lieberman that the two organizations were going to click. That written evidence, backed by AEO's sponsorship of the MTV award, suggested value and mission congruency. In effect, Lieberman did his due diligence on AEO. There was sufficient overlap in target constituencies and resonance between business and social goals to make a case for aligning activities in ways that would benefit both organizations.

Lieberman's instincts proved correct. Kolber reported that Jumpstart brought to the table at the right time many things with which AEO wanted to be connected: inner-city engagement, educational program focus, use of a target consumer group as tutors and mentors. "I didn't go seeking out Jumpstart, but when it fell into my lap," he recalled, "I identified it immediately as being something that was good and that the whole organization thought was good. After we had a full understanding of it we just embraced it." Kolber's increasing personal interaction with Lieberman only enhanced what was a good strategic fit from the start.

The relationship was also facilitated by Lieberman's and Kolber's clarity of vision and articulateness with respect to what their roles ought to be in business, community, and society. Kolber, for example, articulated well-defined ideas about what kind of company he wants AEO to be, what kinds of social causes he wants it to support, and what kinds of partners make sense for AEO in such social enterprises. For his part, Lieberman was clear, articulate, honest, and consistent about Jumpstart's mission and goals. He projected strongly the values of service, remedial intervention, and social change that his organization is committed to uphold and practice. He was also very pragmatic about achieving those goals and about the necessity of viable commercial partnerships that did not compromise Jumpstart's values. This mutual clarity facilitated the partnership creation process by making areas of mission and value overlap more identifiable. Such transparency would be equally useful if an organization were deciding whom not to partner with.

Jumpstart progressed through the philanthropic stage of collaboration by first soliciting free clothing (T-shirts), and then it upped the commitment by asking for cash contributions. But it quickly exited this handout stage and moved along the Collaboration Continuum in order to broaden and deepen the relationship.

Stage Two: Progressive Engagement and Resource Exchange

Other events and interactions during 1997 and 1998 enabled the two organizations to get to know one another better, feel more confident about the potential of the alliance, and discover new ways to produce mutual benefits. A meeting in Pittsburgh in 1998 between AEO officers and the Jumpstart executive team broadened personal interaction and relationships beyond the CEOs to a larger leadership cadre. At the meeting, Lieberman and Hutchison made a successful formal presentation to AEO's leadership team about how, by building on what had already been done, AEO and Jumpstart could take the partnership to the next level.

Lieberman later made the observation that the airfare from Boston to Pittsburgh had represented a significant portion of young Jumpstart's meager travel budget. Accepting that expense was an acknowledgment that early-stage alliance building requires investing risk capital. This particular investment paid big dividends.

Lieberman nurtured the budding alliance by drawing on his relationship network to mobilize reinforcing support. Through his relationship with City Year Lieberman got to know Timberland COO Jeff Swartz, who agreed to speak with Kolber. Lieberman believes the two leaders "really hit it off." Swartz shared his experience with the City Year collaboration and explained how it had afforded Timberland staff an opportunity for community service involvement and commitment. Lieberman viewed the interaction between the AEO and Timberland CEOs as a reversal of the usual business practice of treating competitive practices as proprietary. To the contrary, he reported Swartz's attitude to be one of wide openness, of sharing lessons learned from the experience of partnering with a social change agent such as City Year. Swartz's rationale for this sharing was that "what we're all trying to do is change the world."

Kolber reports that he has kept in touch with Swartz and has discussed how AEO and Timberland might work together on dealing with other inner-city problems. (The two also subsequently explored possible joint business activities.) Kolber and Lieberman thus ended up working off the same City Year–Timberland model in building their own alliance.

By involving AEO in a national forum on education in Washington, D.C., in June 1998, Jumpstart was effectively providing the company access to Jumpstart's network. AEO's relationship with Jumpstart was spotlighted in front of national political and corporate leaders, which helped to further cement that relationship. For AEO, the event's context and its audience of other socially conscious businesses served to further legitimize the kind of partnership Jumpstart was trying to build.

The forum, which included a series of roundtables on strategic corporate partnerships and social change, was in Lieberman's estimation "a world-class event." Another positive step in the progressive engagement between the two partners, the forum constituted a public dialogue about how to make such corporate-nonprofit partnerships work. Corporate and NPO peers publicly reaffirmed the kinds of joint activities Jumpstart and AEO were discussing privately. Lieberman believed that exposing Kolber to this debate would deepen his personal investment in the success of Jumpstart, demonstrate how serious Jumpstart was about the relationship, and strengthen the bonds between the two organizations.

Lieberman also arranged for Kolber to attend, in conjunction with the National Forum on Education, a reception given by Jumpstart's other primary business partner, Hale & Dorr, a Boston law firm. It was helpful for Kolber to hear from other corporate partners about how their relationships were working and what it took to make them effective. Kolber was able to contribute to the roundtable debate (impressively, according to Lieberman) his story about AEO's involvement with Jumpstart. In a sense the event was like the converted preaching to one another: it was a collective alliance laboratory in which participants shared what they had learned (or were learning) about how to effectively manage cross-sector alliances. For Kolber, this novel experience was reinforcing and helped deepen his personal commitment.

The stage of the AEO-Jumpstart interchange was also advanced by the foregoing actions. Instead of continuing in the charitable mode of providing some T-shirts to the preschoolers, AEO proposed that the mentors too have T-shirts and that throughout the year caps and other apparel be added to encourage mentors and preschoolers to identify and bond further with one another. The idea was that making the program more visible would generate pride in the activity and remove any stigma that might be attached to remedial education. In effect, AEO was using its core competencies and products to enhance the effectiveness of Jumpstart's mentoring program.

An ancillary benefit that accrued to AEO was greater corporate visibility through wider use of its branded clothing. The uniforms also (like those supplied by Timberland to City Year) enhanced Jumpstart's visibility and identity. Resource exchange was increasing and becoming two-way.

For Jumpstart's Dawn Hutchison the relationship had migrated to a postcash phase. "Now," she said, "it's about other things that need to grow: professional advice, mentoring, support, access to new markets." Likewise for AEO, the partnership it had cultivated with Jumpstart had become more strategic and longer term than its other philanthropic ventures.

Progress on collaborative undertakings and the personal relationship that had developed between Lieberman and Kolber emboldened Jumpstart to request a $200,000 cash commitment to enable it to implement its strategy of creating a national network for Jumpstart programs. AEO's positive response to this appeal encouraged Lieberman and Hutchison to probe further into other avenues of strategic partnering that would both make good business sense for AEO and further the partners' mutual social goals.

Stage Three: Scaling Up and Organizational Integration

Jumpstart's strategy to scale up into a national network being congruent with AEO's own national expansion strategy, AEO seemed receptive to playing the role of lead sponsor. "Jumpstart is getting an organization that can help them grow," affirmed Kolber. "We're in a lot of cities. They, hopefully, are going to be in a lot of cities. We're going to stand behind them. I've already started networking with other businesses. We have a sister company in Columbus, and they've already jumped on the Jumpstart bandwagon. And we can talk to suppliers. We can provide marketing services and some creativity that they haven't had in the past. It's not only giving cash, not only merchandise. We have the ability to provide a lot of different services, a lot of different thinking, and a lot of networking."

In October 1998, Jumpstart opened in San Francisco. "The corps members pulled on their new Jumpstart AEO T-shirts and were immediately connected with our entire organization and our network," remarked Lieberman. Added Jumpstart board chair Jeff Bradach: "It was just like walking into a room in Boston. You enter, see the shirts, see that activity going on. It was inspiring." Because AEO was particularly interested in increasing its visibility in its headquarters city of Pittsburgh and Jumpstart had received a strong new-site proposal from the University of Pittsburgh, Jumpstart also agreed to launch operations there as part of its national network. The rollout has begun, and the alliance is producing mutual brand-building benefits.

AEO and Jumpstart are also growing closer in their interactions. Personal encounters between the two CEOs are evolving into mutual mentoring, each tutoring the other on the philosophy and pragmatics of the joint enterprise, particularly the importance of results. Emphasizing the contingent connection between corporate commitment and program performance, Kolber assures Lieberman that support is forthcoming "as long as you continue to succeed and you can show the results."

With increasing resource commitment comes increasing accountability. The relationship has moved to an equity investment joint venture, with expected dividends in the form of high social performance. Organizational integration took a further step forward in October 1998 when Kolber became a member of Jumpstart's board of directors.

Jumpstart mentors, Kolber believes, "would be good ambassadors for American Eagle, tell their friends that it is a good company and that it supports Jumpstart. We want to appear positive in the eyes of the consuming public. It's nice to be nice; it's also nice to be known to be nice. We don't want to do this anonymously. We want people to know that we're good citizens." "We are unabashed about saying we are working to help build a better American Eagle brand," adds Lieberman, expressing the hope that AEO will likewise be un-abashed about saying, "We're working to build a better Jumpstart brand." "If you're going to be committed fully," Kolber concurs, "that means you have to use your networking abilities and do things to promote. You have to be the ambassador for Jumpstart." (This early aggressive and proactive stance toward publicly promoting the part-nership contrasts with the initial ambiguity and hesitancy observed in the City Year–Timberland and CARE-Starbucks alliances.)

Although they are just entering this next level of engagement, Jumpstart and AEO have reached it in a very short period of time. The trajectory promises to take them rapidly into deeper, richer, more complicated collaboration.

Alliance Drivers

Experience to date suggests that the primary driving forces that have energized the rapid development of the AEO-Jumpstart alliance are alignment of mission, strategy, and values; personal connections and relationships; and value creation.

Mission, Strategy, and Values Alignment

The deep strategic fit between the organizations serves various purposes for both organizations in marketing and brand identification, in broadening the service base from regional to national levels, in developing an image of social engagement, and in providing opportunities for community involvement that tie the organizations' missions together.

Timing was a factor in effecting a good strategic fit. Jumpstart effectively catalyzed a change in the nature and direction of AEO's involvement with nonprofits. Kolber observed that during the period leading up to the Jumpstart alliance the company had already begun to question how to go beyond its traditional giving to charities and how to identify the right nonprofit with which to become involved in more meaningful and effective ways. Jumpstart opened doors to social causes (such as inner-city children and education) with which AEO wanted to be associated and provided opportunities that made good business sense as well.

But being a corporate force for social change requires access to funds, a resource that is critically dependent on business performance. Kolber recalled AEO's changing fortunes over the last three years, from fighting for its existence to surviving to become a strong, viable, industry leader. As its fortunes changed, so did its priorities.

When things were tough and there was a lot of turnover, survival had been the only priority; philanthropy and partnering with non-profits were not high on the agenda. But with better times had come the means to implement a broader corporate philosophy, and the company's social agenda reemerged. (These struggles echoed Star-bucks' fight for existence before it was able to engage with CARE.)

"We recognized over that three-year period," Kolber reflected, "that once you fight for survival and you make it, you have a duty to give something back to the community." Consequently, AEO became interested in developing a vision of community outreach and involvement that would link the company to the larger social order in which it operated and also engage the goodwill of its employees in community service related to their work. "People need to feel good about the organization they represent, and that happens when an organization is doing well," Kolber observed. "Furthermore, we have 350 stores, and those people, given the opportunity, would love to participate in a program. . . . It brings a lot of people in different segments of the company together."

The close alignment of the organizations' target constituencies—namely, the college-age group that is AEO's prime customer base and the pool of volunteers for Jumpstart's preschooler tutoring program—was another facilitator of the union between AEO and Jumpstart. Kolber readily identified mutual benefits that would flow from AEO's involvement, via product and cash donations, with Jumpstart's preschool and college-age clients and programs. "This is a mentoring program using college kids who are our core customers," he explained. "They could help other young adults identify with us."

Also contributing to the timing and goodness of fit was AEO's renewed business growth and expansion during this period, which enabled the partners to leverage one another's strengths in the areas of marketing and brand expansion. As AEO's business exploded, it began to develop as a national brand, which coincided with Jumpstart's strategy to develop a national brand image for its programs.

AEO further refined its market niche to target a population of college students and graduates very similar in profile to Jumpstart corps members.

Jumpstart's statement of mission and vision resonated in a very timely manner with a reassessment of corporate goals at an important stage in AEO's evolution, illustrating how being able even to articulate a social goal, let alone accomplish it, is deterministically intertwined with a company's business performance. The experience also attests to some enduring qualities of AEO's societal vision, which primed the company to take full advantage of what Jumpstart had to offer when the opportunity arose. In an important way Jumpstart gave voice to the social values, mission, and vision AEO was trying to formulate.

As in many successful collaborations, a shared voice helped to rationalize and reinforce motive. When Kolber described the mission and vision his company wanted to develop, the goodness of fit with Jumpstart became even more apparent. Besides the obvious business benefit of affording access to a college-age consumer population, the Jumpstart connection helped AEO accomplish a set of job enrichment and corporate value objectives. As it became more internally diverse, AEO wanted to be associated with programs that would promote a parallel diversity on the outside and help it participate in outreach to inner cities and minorities. This would demonstrate not just a corporate commitment to diversity but might also tangibly engage AEO employees in community efforts to better the larger society. "We're good matches for each other, and we saw that right away," declared Lieberman. "We have continued to explore the relationship knowing that's our common ground."

Personal Connections and Relationships

Individuals are the architects, builders, and sustainers of organizational partnerships. Cross-sector collaborations are fueled by personal commitment to the social mission and cemented by strong personal relationships across the organizations. Sustainability relies on strong commitment and good chemistry at the top level and, ultimately, throughout the organization.

Kolber was receptive to Jumpstart because his executive team had endorsed the organization. That he embraced it so wholeheartedly was due to the personal connection he could make with the mission. "One of the things with Jumpstart that hit me was that I grew up in an immigrant foster family," Kolber reminisced. "And, quite honestly, I struggled with reading early on. So I sort of connected with Jumpstart's mission right away on a personal level."

As peers, Lieberman and Kolber soon discovered that they shared a common vision and goals about childhood education and also about corporations' involvement in community betterment. Shared values are fertile terrain for growing a healthy relationship, but the personal dynamic is a determining variable. "You have to like the people you're dealing with," Kolber insisted. "If the people turn you off, I don't care how good the cause is, it doesn't make any difference." The positive personal chemistry between Kolber and Lieberman seems to have spread to others in their organizations.

A unique value that Hutchison would like to maintain in the ongoing personal relations is to make every phone call between the partners count: "I would like to think," she reflected, "that every time they get off the phone with Jumpstart . . . they're inspired by our commitment, they're inspired by their own commitment to the organization, and that's what drives them to continue to move forward in the relationship. That's something we can bring in a way that another partner can't."

The leadership connection and organizational integration deepened when Kolber was named to Jumpstart's board of directors (the same important connection made by City Year, CARE, and The Nature Conservancy with their business partners). Incorporating the corporate partner into the nonprofit's governance structure might be seen by some as ceding control and undue influence to the corporation, but seldom do corporate leaders seek out such positions. The initiative is usually that of the NPO. Such appointments signal great trust and deepen the personal commitment of the corporate partner.

The network of relationships in the AEO-Jumpstart alliance has now expanded beyond the CEOs. Early on, Kolber made it clear that the alliance would work only if Lieberman were able to get other company managers to buy into the partnership. It was an AEO-created company foundation, run by four members of the management executive committee, that selected Jumpstart as its major programmatic initiative. This broadened engagement was evident in the spring of 1999, when foundation chair Susan Miller and several headquarters managers joined with store managers in Boston to participate with great enthusiasm in Jumpstart's KidsFest, a day-long event that involved more than one thousand parents, children, and volunteers in a wide variety of literacy-based learning activities. "Being there was very powerful," recalled Miller. "There is an infectious kind of excitement when you are experiencing it side by side with the children. We also saw how significant an organization Jumpstart was in Boston." Personal emotional connection derived from service experience is a powerful motivator.

Value Creation

The cash and in-kind donations and good feelings and positive publicity exchanged in philanthropic stage relationships are *generic* in that they could come from most partners. Whereas many collaborations stay at this relatively low level of value exchange, their strategic perspective and entrepreneurialism propelled AEO and Jumpstart to envision and seek to generate higher levels of value.

Kolber looked to AEO's social engagement to foster organizational unity among the company's various parts. The unifying common bond he sought was provided by Jumpstart's mission to children and education, to which everyone in AEO could relate. Asserted Kolber: "Store people are store people; merchants are merchants; warehouse people are warehouse people. But if they all participate in Jumpstart, they're all Jumpstart people!"

Kolber sees the alliance with Jumpstart as organizational glue that creates a shared involvement that has a positive impact on employees' lives, on the life of the company, and on society. Jump-start satisfied a need perceived by Kolber among his employees: "People want to help . . . they . . . appreciate something that they can do and that they feel good about."

Beyond these internal benefits tied to shared belief in Jumpstart's mission are pragmatic market enhancement benefits such as culti-vating AEO's target customer group and developing its brand image, goals that in fact coincide nicely for both partners. AEO is strong in retailing, product design, and promotion, areas in which Lieber-man confesses to be weak. For his part, Lieberman insisted that AEO optimize the business advantages of the collaboration by exploiting Jumpstart's strengths in reaching and interacting with youth. Because the partners are tapping their core competencies, the value of the alliance's resource exchange is enhanced.

A sense of each partner caring about the other, expressed as a concern about what makes good business sense for the other, seems to be a salient feature of the relationship between Kolber and Lieberman. Just as AEO genuinely wants Jumpstart's activities and programmatic goals to be good vehicles for channeling the com-pany's efforts, energies, time, and money, so Lieberman genuinely hopes that Jumpstart can help AEO to "try to get involved in really meaningful and powerful ways to leverage the most for what they're doing in communities." That each partner is concerned about cre-ating value for the other has helped to ensure a two-way value ex-change and balance in the transactions. (Conversely, the value inequality that attends a significant imbalance in a resource exchange can lead to deterioration of interest in continuing to invest in a partnership.)

It was precisely this kind of mutuality paradigm that proved so attractive to AEO and so preferable to what other charities' alliance proposals offered. In the new partnership paradigm advanced by Jumpstart, the collaborators would work together to discover new ways to combine their competencies to achieve mutually beneficial results. This openness and entrepreneurial attitude moved the partners from mere resource exchange toward joint creation of value. To the extent that the partners are able to meld their capabilities synergistically to generate distinctive activities and outcomes, the collaboration's value construct, being uniquely due to the alliance and not attainable separately or through other partnerships, will have moved to a higher level.

The AEO-Jumpstart alliance being relatively young, the social value it will produce is mostly still to come. It appears that it will take the form largely of scale enhancement, reflected in the way it has enabled the Jumpstart program to go national. Although Jumpstart is drawing support from other partners for this effort, networking through AEO's chain of stores and with its business contacts and using the company's marketing expertise and the uniforms it provides are proving to be invaluable aids. Thousands more preschoolers will be assisted because of this collaborative effort. And (as with the City Year–Timberland alliance) secondary social benefits accrue to Jumpstart's tutors and AEO's employee volunteers: greater individual psychic income, a heightened sense of community solidarity, and an enhanced appreciation for social diversity.

Alliance Enablers

Behind these drivers that provide the primary power to the alliance are additional supportive factors, or enablers. Threaded through the interactions that sustain partnering on a week-to-week, month-to-month basis are processes that clarify purpose and focus attention, foster mutual expectations, and facilitate value creation through ongoing communication.

Clear Purpose and Focused Attention

Lieberman does not mince words when communicating Jumpstart's purpose to potential partners. It is this sense of clear purpose that enables him to get his message of social change across in terms that are unambiguous. "What we're selling," he maintains, "is a chance to get involved with an incredible solution to a pressing problem. That's the only resource that we have at the end of the day. People want that. People are willing to pay money for that because they think it's right."

Lieberman's clarity of purpose is consistent with Hutchison's insistence that each phone call be inspiring. Both executives are savvy enough to know that complacency sounds the death knell to ongoing relationships and that momentum is maintained through discipline. This exercise in continual self-definition expresses their purpose and helps keep their attention focused. Remaining clear and focused about Jumpstart's image also projects to existing and potential partners alike what Jumpstart stands for—and what it will not do. It will not, for example, accept contributions from alcohol or tobacco companies. It seeks partners with which it can generate value that supports its mission to children, families, and schooling.

Jumpstart's clear statement of purpose provides a unique focus of attention for AEO and one that Kolber buys into. It opens doorways for business and marketing ventures in ways that enable the business partner to participate in meaningful social intervention and change. The resulting participation and engagement at many levels of the company is life enhancing at both the institutional and personal levels. "Both sides having specific goals is what really accelerated our relationship," observed Miller. "And Kolber's emphasis on results, in turn, helps maintain and focus Jumpstart's attention on what it takes to survive in the competitive world of cross-sector alliance building. AEO has moved (like Timberland with City Year), to see its relationship with Jumpstart as the primary focus of its social engagement." Added Kolber, "We will do things for other organizations, but I think the long-term, full-time commitment will be to Jumpstart." The strategic decision to have a single primary social partner enables AEO to concentrate its resources so as to develop a deeply intensive relationship.

Mutual Expectations

These partners expect high performance from each other, but each actively seeks ways to bring value from the alliance to the other partner. They visibly champion each other and their partnership.

One important element that AEO brings to the expectation equation is an emphasis on results and accountability for performance. Kolber likes being involved with an enterprise that "shows real accountability, shows that there is a goal out there, that we're expanding and we're affecting more lives." Jumpstart's funding is tied to its ability to grow and enroll more corps members. Kolber wants to make sure that the alliance is given a chance and enough time so the company will be able to judge its success or failure on proper grounds. Hence the expectations Kolber sets reflect an investor perspective. "For me to embrace anything," he stresses, "I want to see that it affects a lot of people, that I get a lot of bang for the buck. If you just want to give money, that's fine. But you cannot hold people to the degree of accountability that I will because of our level of commitment to Jumpstart." The larger the resources, the deeper the commitment, the greater the accountability.

Mutual expectations need to be recalibrated from time to time as relationships broaden and deepen and other forms of strategic cooperation are contemplated. Lieberman believes that the onus is on AEO "not to assume that the solutions that work in their business would work in ours." Jumpstart tries to do likewise when it counsels AEO about how proposed strategic initiatives connect it to the bigger social picture.

Communication Processes

Lieberman and Kolber have had good communication from day one of their relationship. Although necessarily brief, this communication has continued to be frequent. Other AEO and Jumpstart staff have also interacted, but it has been the direct personal communication between the two CEOs that has driven the collaboration.

Such personal involvement has reinforced their willingness to commit organizational resources.

The mutual respect and trust engendered by the warm personal relations between Lieberman and Kolber have further facilitated the communication process. The partners have worked together to communicate information about the alliance to their constituencies. Lieberman joined AEO's top management in announcing to headquarters' staff the rollout of the company's foundation and its support of Jumpstart. In June 1999, at the annual AEO stores conference, Lieberman worked with regional and district managers to develop ideas for ways AEO employees might volunteer in Jumpstart activities. Lieberman anticipated that a benefit party for Jumpstart hosted by AEO in conjunction with the opening in San Francisco of its first California store would "dramatically increase the visibility of Jumpstart's San Francisco program." Remarked Miller, "This partnership is still in its infancy, but already in the organization there is a sense of pride in the relationship."

Kolber makes it clear that AEO is impressed with the manner in which Jumpstart communicated its mission and vision. It is seen to differ from other charitable ventures in its ability to communicate not only a duty but an ideal. Jumpstart executives are perceived to have "a want and desire more than a sense of obligation." Lieberman and Hutchison, although they believe that the communication process still requires a lot of homework, are nevertheless scoring top marks with Kolber and AEO. The two are served well by their ability to communicate belief in their cause with enthusiasm and energy, a proactive attitude, and a desire that the partnership make a difference. Kolber believes alliance partners able to share the same vision "and work off the same page" impart power to collaboration.

Jumpstart leaders' ability to use the language and vocabulary of the corporate partner to sell and communicate a shared vision resulted in a strategic focus on results that could give investors the message that AEO was buying change when it bought into the Jumpstart model. At a time when Kolber and AEO were starting to think strategically about how to get more out of their social involve-ment, Lieberman's vision convinced them that dollars invested in Jumpstart programs would have high impact and leverage, affecting the lives of preschoolers with consequent lifelong benefits. "We came to apply the same business savvy they applied to earning their money to giving it away," Lieberman explains. Effective cross-sector com-munication typically reflects just such bilingualism.

Alliance Challenges

Among the challenges Jumpstart and AEO have faced as they have moved progressively through the stages of engagement are those related to management of the relationship, value definition, and brand creation and dissemination.

Communication and Relationship Management

Even as their personal relations with Kolber have deepened, Hutchison and Lieberman have understood that collaboration must spread more broadly throughout the AEO organization and have taken advantage of recent joint marketing proposals to begin work-ing more closely with AEO's design department to develop new clothing products for Jumpstart. Spreading the interaction between the partners has generated new excitement among the staff on both sides. For Jumpstart and AEO staff to do more together on an oper-ational level, the partners must map out additional communication channels so that the CEOs do not necessarily need to be the main communicators. Seeing the effects of interaction spreading through-out his company, Kolber is optimistic that his people will get the job done. Already a certain amount of administrative support is be-ing provided to Jumpstart by AEO, and discussions about how to broaden the channels of communication and get more AEO employees involved are ongoing. Employees might receive credit or time off for participating in the promotion of Jumpstart's mentor-ing programs, for example. Beyond such in-house initiatives, Kolber is beginning to explore other ways to leverage the relationship, such as by spreading the word about Jumpstart's programs through vendors and suppliers.

Even with intentions and goals so well aligned on both sides of the partnership, Kolber and Lieberman agree that time and time management remain the biggest obstacles and constraints on the collaboration's rate of progress. Lieberman believes that time constraints represent a challenge in terms of prioritization and of conceptualization of operational details.

Hutchison, who would love to invest time brainstorming with AEO staff about the future of the relationship, points to an important lesson Jumpstart has learned about the connection between communication and integrity. She believes that nonprofit–for-profit partnerships require "incredible communication, for your corporate partner has to understand what your goals are . . . and you need to stick to those goals, and everything that that partnership brings should be furthering your goals in addition to their goals." AEO's Susan Miller believes firmly that Jumpstart has done a good job communicating that integrity: "Aaron Lieberman is just so sincere and he works so hard. We respect him deeply."

Brand Dissemination

From Jumpstart's perspective, brand identity and brand promotion represent opportunities rather than problems. AEO's business expansion to a national level coincides with Jumpstart's plans to grow a national network and build a Jumpstart brand that has greater leverage and return for potential sponsors. This expansion in turn can become a vehicle for market access by AEO, which can piggyback on the Jumpstart brand dissemination to market AEO products. The challenge at the moment is not how to protect one's brand (as it might be in other partnerships) but how to be creative about using brand dissemination to build the relationship even further. For instance, recent discussions have explored the possibility of developing a cobranded product that could be sold through AEO stores or of driving sales via comerchandising on AEO's Web site, with some of the profits directed to Jumpstart.

AEO is also keen to promote the Jumpstart brand nationally, Kolber vowing that his company "will stand behind" Jumpstart's efforts to expand its programs nationally. He has begun to network with other businesses on Jumpstart's behalf and believes that AEO can provide creativity and marketing services for brand dissemination to which Jumpstart has not had access in the past.

Value Creation

Keenly aware of the ongoing challenge to preserve the value of the mutual benefit flow, Lieberman strives to maintain a running dialogue with his corporate partner about whether or not Jumpstart's proposals make good business sense for AEO. He characterizes this as "trying to figure out how to help create the change that we all want to see come about, and at the same time build the value for that business, because if times get tough, business's funds become scarcer." Lieberman seems to recognize that whereas philanthropy is the motivator that gets the partner in the door, it is the pragmatics of creating value that drives the relationship.

Jumpstart tries actively to encourage AEO to think in terms of how theirs can be a strategic business partnership in the context of a philanthropic endeavor. Jumpstart continues to draw upon the example of Timberland to educate Kolber about how their joint enterprise might become part of AEO's organizational culture.

On AEO's side, a major value is getting access to a constituency of socially conscious young adults whom AEO cares very much about as consumers. It is Jumpstart's ability to bring AEO access to people and promotional opportunities that it could not get anywhere else that is making this a win-win situation for both partners. Kolber's take on this is that the partnership creates value via different kinds of *bonding:* the bonding between the Jumpstart preschooler and his college student mentor, which might further translate into bonding between that mentor and a sponsor company such as AEO; the bonding that occurs among employees in different parts of the company as they all help Jumpstart; the bonding that develops between employees and the company as a consequence of corporate support for Jumpstart; and the similar bonding between corporate headquarters and the field store staff. Kolber also emphasizes the critical relationship between opportunities for community service and the company's charity investment decisions, which drives AEO to partner in ways that will create value and serve corporate needs. Among the questions he asks are: "How will it affect our own employees? Does it bring people together? Is it something that all of our employees can share in?"

Conclusion

That Jumpstart and AEO have progressed so far along the Collaboration Continuum in such a relatively short span of time speaks largely to the auspicious beginnings of their partnership, in which timing and goodness of fit played key roles. The alliance drivers and enablers contributing to the continued maturation of this alliance include strategic fit, shared vision, personal connection, value creation, focused attention, mutual expectations, trust, and communication. Underlying these factors is the leapfrogging along the Collaboration Continuum that the partners were able to do as a result of learning from and modeling their efforts after the City Year–Timberland alliance.

Board chair Jeffrey Bradach summarizes the importance of Jumpstart's alliance with AEO: "This is extremely important to us not just for the financial resources, although these are vital because they reduce our dependency on government funding. Their staff has helped us with training, growth strategy, and introductions to other companies. It is a deep relationship. They understand us and are there for us when we need them. This represents a partnering model for us. Deepening this relationship even further and multiplying other alliances are essential to our sustainability and growth."

To a large extent this particular partnering process represents a dialogue and debate about social change and the means to effect it through the collaborative application of cross-sector expertise. Jumpstart is extremely conscious of actively cultivating an open and learning relationship with AEO that will stand the test of time. In their continuing dialogue the partners have been willing to learn and speak a common language of change. Their lateral learning and joint creativity bodes well for the continued evolution of this young but fruitful partnership. So too does their depth of mutual commitment, revealed in Kolber's summary piece of partnering advice: "If you're going to collaborate, be committed 100 percent. Make sure you give it a chance; make sure you give it some time; and don't do anything halfway, because then you're never going to be able to judge your success or failure. If you want to get involved, get completely involved."

8

Guidelines for Collaborating Successfully

Creating and developing strategic alliances between nonprofits and corporations involves entrepreneurial and managerial challenges of the highest order. Successfully meeting those challenges earns commensurate rewards. Assuming that there are simple, standard steps that one can rigidly follow cloaks the inherent complexity of partnering and courts disaster. Effective collaboration ultimately involves jointly tailoring a garment that fits the unique characteristics and needs of the partners. This chapter keeps this imperative clearly in mind as it synthesizes from the previous chapters a set of guidelines for those who would build alliances between the nonprofit and corporate worlds. I call these guidelines to cross-sector alliance the *seven C's of strategic collaboration*. Exhibit 8.1, at the end of the chapter, offers a consolidated checklist of questions for organizations applying the seven C's guidelines.

CONNECTION with Purpose and People

Purpose and people are primary in the collaborations we have examined. Alliances are successful when key individuals connect personally and emotionally with the alliance's social purpose and with each other.

Serendipity often prevails as the initiator of connections in the alliance marketplace, which is still maturing, but connections are more readily made among organizations predisposed to partner and alert and prepared to seize opportunities. Systematic searches can target potential partner organizations that appear to have shared interests, appropriate operations, or track records in the social arena. Investing up front in getting to know key individuals in a prospective partner organization is an essential part of the due diligence required to assess interorganizational compatibility, character, and competency. Getting acquainted at the individual level pays cooperation and commitment dividends later. Positive personal chemistry is essential to productive partnerships even though not sufficient alone to guarantee alliance success, whereas bad interpersonal relations alone can destroy a partnership.

Passion is the motivational driver and inspiration a key currency in cross-sector collaboration. Strategic collaborations need champions, or internal entrepreneurs (*intrapreneurs*), at high levels on both sides. The engagement of and relationships between top leaders of the corporation and the nonprofit largely determine the acceptance and vigor of the collaboration. Leadership's initial challenge is to engage and nurture the relationship, its subsequent challenge to transcend the top-level link. On the business side, directly exposing individuals to and involving them in the social service activity often deepens their motivation and personal connection. Similarly, on the nonprofit side, exposing individuals to the business's operations promotes greater understanding of the partner and its relevant capabilities. Creating opportunities for interaction and service engagement by employees at all levels in both organizations fosters personal relationships and connection with the cause.

In seeking a new connection or assessing an existing one, nonprofits and businesses alike need to consider the following questions:

- To what extent are individuals personally and emotionally connected to the social purpose of the collaboration?

- Have individuals been able to *touch, feel,* and *see* the social value of the collaboration?

- What level and what quality of interaction exist among senior leaders?

- To what extent do personal connections and inter-actions occur at other levels across the partnering organizations?

- How strong are interpersonal bonds?

CLARITY of Purpose

Above all, collaborators need to be clear about the purpose of joint undertakings. Because of the social goodness of these projects, busi-nesspeople sometimes are lax in setting clear objectives, when exactly the opposite is needed. The rigor and discipline that com-panies apply to clearly targeted business investments are also vital to the crafting of social purpose partnerships. Vagueness or ambiguity will cloud the vision of the undertaking and may breed confusion or even conflict. To help ensure clarity of purpose, prospective partners should jointly prepare a written collaboration purpose statement. As both the processes and the end product (the statement) can benefit a partnership, it is important that the partners be explicit about what they expect to take from their relationship. Partners should also identify where on the Collaboration Continuum a proposed or exist-ing relationship falls and where they would like it to fall.

Specific, limited collaborative projects often serve a useful pur-pose and may be all either party is ready to undertake. But when the objective is to achieve higher-value strategic collaborations, both parties need to abandon traditional, narrow mind-sets. Nonprofits need to escape the gratefulness syndrome, the supplicant mentality often common to traditional philanthropic relationships. As illus-trated repeatedly in the previous chapters, nonprofits bring to the collaboration table significant assets that are value-adding oppor-tunities for corporate partners. Corporations in turn must get be-yond the charity syndrome if their engagements with nonprofits are to become strategically central to their business operations. A collaboration mind-set supplants the *them and us* perspective with a *we together* perspective.

With the growing proclivity to engage in multiple collaborations, it is useful for organizations to think in terms of a *collaboration portfolio*. This involves clarifying the purposes and relative importance of existing collaborative relationships and using that information as the basis for establishing the number and mix of alliances that collectively will contribute most productively to the organization's mission.

The following questions can help organizations ensure that clarity of purpose guides their decisions about partners to court and types of collaboration to pursue:

- What is the purpose of the collaboration?

- Where does the relationship fall on the Collaboration Continuum (philanthropic, transactional, or integrative), and where does each partner want it to be?

- Have the partners escaped the gratefulness and charity syndromes?

- Do both partners have written collaboration purpose statements?

- Has each partner determined the different functions and relative importance of the partnerships already existing in its collaboration portfolio?

CONGRUENCY of Mission, Strategy, and Values

As an extension of clarifying purpose, partnering organizations should identify areas of alignment between their missions, strategies, and values. Engaging early in conversations about alignment is essential to building a solid foundation for collaboration. The closer the alignment, the greater the potential gains from collaboration. Overlap is more likely than total congruency, but where fit is largely or completely lacking, collaboration is ill advised.

The point where two organizations' missions mesh becomes an arena of collaborative action. Discovering all the productive intersections of mission fit often requires careful scrutiny. Taking time to experiment often reveals valuable new opportunities for collaboration, as the many examples of productive joint endeavors described in the preceding chapters testify. It is healthy to grow relationships incrementally, moreover, because experience unveils new possibilities.

The potential internal impact of collaboration increases with the accumulation of experience and interaction. As alliances evolve, they can influence even the partners' definitions of their respective missions and values, which in turn can lead to new areas of overlap and engagement. As external forces can undermine this growing cohesiveness, giving rise to misalignments, continual scrutiny is warranted. Shared visioning of future fit helps ensure continuing congruency and can broaden the existing fit. The more aligned a collaboration's purpose with the partners' respective missions and strategies, the more sustainable the alliance is likely to be in the face of transitory storms that afflict one partner or the other.

The following considerations are relevant to the pursuit of strategic fit:

- How well does each partner understand the other's business?

- What are the missions, strategies, and values of each partner?

- What are the areas of current and potential overlap?

- How can each partner help the other accomplish its mission?

- To what extent is the collaboration a strategic tool for each partner?

- Have the partners engaged in shared visioning about future fit?

CREATION of Value

High-performance collaborations are about much more than giving and receiving money. They are about mobilizing and combining multiple resources and capabilities to generate benefits for both partners and social value for society. Partners need to systematically focus on *defining, generating, balancing,* and *renewing value*. The Collaboration Value Construct (Chapter Five) provides a means for both partners to jointly and explicitly specify the benefits they expect to obtain from collaboration. Do not assume that your interests will be implicitly known by your partner or that your partner's interests will be implicitly known by you. Partners are well advised to ask continually what they can do for one another and to avoid fixating on what their partner is going to do for them.

Collaboration is an ongoing search for value that can be created by partners jointly but not by one organization alone. The highest value is realized when the organizations' core capabilities and resources are deployed to produce benefits that cannot be obtained from any other alliance. This result is the distinctive collaborative advantage of the partnership. In addition to specifying respective expected benefits, each partner should also indicate the incremental social value that the alliance is expected to create. Multiparty alliances can generate multiple value creation opportunities.

For alliances to retain their vitality and mutual engagement, benefit flows must be two-way and relatively balanced. Knowing when they are balanced is complicated by the fact that individual partner's benefits differ in kind and weighting. Unlike commercial partnerships' benefits, which are often reducible to monetary terms, cross-sector alliances deal in multiple currencies, some of which are difficult to quantify. Consequently, it is important that partners consult about whether net benefit flows are adequate and balanced. A sense of equitable reciprocity is essential to partners' continuing interest in investing in the relationship. A significant imbalance risks creating excessive dependency or subjecting one partner to undue influence from the other.

Finally, it is important to recognize that collaboration configurations are depreciable assets, that the value of partnering can decline over time. Renewing value is thus an ever-present challenge. As resources always have alternative uses, either in other collaborations or in commercial business activities, it is incumbent on partners to assess periodically the opportunity costs of their participation in a cross-sector alliance. Constant attention to the value generation process and to identifying new avenues of collaboration that might produce both mutual benefits and higher levels of social good are essential to value renewal. Value renewal can be facilitated through periodic strategic visioning exercises in which the partners collectively consider the possible future path and benefit opportunities of the collaboration. Sometimes, however, changes in the internal or external circumstances of one or both partners will so dramatically alter the calculus of the value construct that the alliance will need to be either drastically reformulated or terminated. Knowing when to end a collaborative alliance is as important as knowing when to begin it.

Organizations assessing the worth of a potential or existing alliance should answer the following questions related to generating value:

- What resources of each partner are of value to the other?

- What specific benefits will accrue to each partner from the collaboration?

- Do benefits outweigh costs and risks?

- What social value can be generated by the alliance?

- What new resources, capabilities, and benefits can be created by the collaboration?

- Are resource and capability transfer two-way?

- Are benefits equitably balanced between the partners?

- Has the value exchange and creation depreciated? If so, to what extent?

- Can the Collaboration Value Construct be renewed and enhanced?

- Is it time to end the collaboration?

COMMUNICATION Between Partners

Even in the presence of good personal relations and emotional connections, strategic fit, and successful value creation, a partnership is without a solid foundation if it lacks an effective ongoing communication process. Good communication is essential to building trust, and trust is the intangible that makes a collaboration cohesive. To develop mutual respect and trust takes time, effort, and action. Trust also presupposes a genuine appreciation by the partners for each other's activities. Communication should be honest, forthright, frequent, and meaningful. The power of openness in social purpose collaborations, particularly in integrative stage relationships, is in evidence in the examples in the earlier chapters. Constructive criticism should be welcome but is possible only in open and supportive relationships. A good rule is to never surprise your partner; involve one another early on in the planning for all actions that affect the partnership. Resist the temptation to withdraw in the event of a crisis in either organization. Instead, intensify communication, particularly if the situation might adversely affect the reputation or relationship of the partners.

Multiple connections and communication channels across partnering organizations are desirable. It is also important to assign responsibility for managing the relationship. Strategic partnerships are high-maintenance relationships that require focused attention. If an alliance is truly strategic, each organization will have an assigned partner relationship manager. Having such counterparts can enhance coordination in programs and communication, particularly in the joint formulation of a strategy for communicating about the partnership both internally and externally.

Communication with the world at large about a collaboration is just as important as communication between partners. Hesitancy to overpublicize a partnership frequently results in foregone benefits. An alliance that is truly strategic and progressing into the organizational integration stage should be proudly promoted internally and externally. Reluctance to do so should call into question the solidity of the relationship. It is also vital to ensure that both partners have articulated explicit communication strategies for their internal constituencies and that each is aware of the content and process of the others' communication. Frequent communication about the benefits of an alliance motivates continued collaboration.

Answering the following questions will move partners toward effective communications:

- What level of respect and trust exists between the partners?

- Is communication open and frank, and is critical communication constructive?

- How is communication between the partners managed?

- Does each partner have a partner relationship manager?

- What channels and vehicles are used to communicate internally?

- Are there potential dissenters, and can they be converted?

- How does the alliance communicate externally?

- Do the partners have a coordinated external communication strategy and program?

- Is the partnership underpublicized?

CONTINUAL Learning

Collaboration must be viewed as dynamic. Although systematic analysis and planning are desirable, a partnership's evolution cannot be completely planned or entirely predicted. Partners should view alliances as learning laboratories and cultivate a discovery ethic that supports continual learning.

Continual learning is what enables continuous improvement. Because cross-sector collaboration is still relatively novel, invention and innovation continue to stand in for standard practice. Discovering both the *what* and the *how* of collaboration is also important. Learning about one another's businesses and operations not only builds rapport and enhances communication between partners but can also lead to the identification of new collaboration opportunities. Alliances that combine the distinctive competencies and complementary missions of corporations and nonprofits are opening up new frontiers for generating mutual and exceptional benefits and are simultaneously addressing targeted societal needs more effectively than before. A growing capacity to collaborate is a distinct competency and a competitive advantage that can foster further cross-sector as well as same-sector alliances.

Beyond learning how to collaborate, each partner gains specific valuable skills and knowledge. A nonprofit, for example, might develop marketing, financial, or business-planning skills; its business partner might acquire knowledge of a target group of consumers, new organizational or employee motivational methods, or community relations skills. Employees engaged in community service projects might hone their leadership or teamwork capabilities. The mutual learning benefits of collaboration are many and represent another payoff from partnering.

Partners seeking to leverage learning should consider the following questions:

- What has each partner learned from the collaboration about how to work with another organization more effectively and create greater partner and social value?
- How has this learning been incorporated into the collaboration?
- Is there a process for routinely assessing learning from the collaboration?
- Is complacency stifling innovation?

COMMITMENT to the Partnership

Because partnerships increase in scope, scale, strategic importance, and operational complexity as they advance along the Collaboration Continuum, partners must be prepared to ratchet up their personal, institutional, and resource commitments accordingly. A strategic alliance being a deep relationship, not a deal, partners should take a long-term perspective. Short-term alliances can be useful but tend to be more tactical than strategic.

Sustainable alliances institutionalize their collaboration process. They weave incentives to collaborate into their personnel systems and embed them in the organizational culture. Moreover, as insurance against the exit of key individuals, they ensure continuity by empowering all levels of the organization.

High-performance alliances are driven by high mutual expectations with concomitant mutual accountability. Viewing collaborations as joint ventures with shared equity investments creates an expectation of returns, most fundamentally social impact but also all the other benefits that accrue to partnering organizations. The more explicit the performance assessment, the more likely the collaboration is to focus its collective energies on enhancing impact.

High expectations motivate performance, but it is important to ensure that organizational capabilities are compatible with commitments. Partners should assess whether an execution gap exists and remedy it by mobilizing needed resources or adjusting commitments to realizable levels. This also raises the issue of how many such partnerships collaborating entities should have. Organizations should assess their collaboration capacity, taking into consideration alliances' varying levels of maintenance and resource exchange. To ensure that key relationships are not neglected, organizations should compile their collaboration portfolios with some care. Overcommitting and underdelivering can destroy partner credibility and neglect can lead quickly to partner disengagement.

The following questions are useful in assessing the adequacy of partnering commitment:

- What is the level of organizational commitment to the partnership and how is this commitment demonstrated?

- What is the trend in investments (personal, financial, institutional) in the partnership?

- Are the partners' expectations of one another high?

- Are partner expectations and commitments commensurate with execution capabilities?

- What is the composition of each partner's collaboration portfolio, and where does this alliance fit within those portfolios?

- Are the portfolios consistent with the partners' collaboration capacities?

Toward the Future

Cross-sector collaborations will grow at an increasing rate. These alliances between nonprofits and corporations hold considerable potential for enhancing business and nonprofit performance and for generating social value. This book has tapped the world of practice to glean insights that will deepen our understanding of the partnering process and its many challenges. It is hoped that the conceptual framework and analyses will provide helpful guidance to corporate and nonprofit leaders striving to develop and manage high-performance alliances. Additionally, it is hoped that this research will spur other academics to explore this important social enterprise arena. The age of alliances is upon us. For those with vision and entrepreneurial spirit, the path of social purpose partnering will lead to mutual gains and produce significant benefits for society.

Exhibit 8.1. The Seven C's: Questions for Partners.

CONNECTION with purpose and people	• To what extent are individuals personally and emotionally connected to the social purpose of the collaboration? • Have individuals been able to *touch, feel,* and *see* the social value of the collaboration? • What level and what quality of interaction exist among senior leaders? • To what extent do personal connections and interactions occur at other levels across the partnering organizations? • How strong are interpersonal bonds?
CLARITY of purpose	• What is the purpose of the collaboration? • Where does the relationship fall on the Collaboration Continuum (philanthropic, transactional, or integrative), and where does each partner want it to be? • Have the partners escaped the gratefulness and charity syndromes? • Do both partners have written collaboration purpose statements? • Has each partner determined the different functions and relative importance of the partnerships already existing in its collaboration portfolio?
CONGRUENCY of mission, strategy, and values	• How well does each partner understand the other's business? • What are the missions, strategies, and values of each partner? • What are the areas of current and potential overlap? • How can each partner help the other accomplish its mission? • To what extent is the collaboration a strategic tool for each partner? • Have the partners engaged in shared visioning about future fit?

Exhibit 8.1. The Seven C's: Questions for Partners, Cont'd.

CREATION of value	• What resources of each partner are of value to the other? • What specific benefits will accrue to each partner from the collaboration? • Do benefits outweigh costs and risks? • What social value can be generated by the alliance? • What new resources, capabilities, and benefits can be created by the collaboration? • Are resource and capability transfer two-way? • Are benefits equitably balanced between the partners? • Has the value exchange and creation depreciated? If so, to what extent? • Can the Collaboration Value Construct be renewed and enhanced? • Is it time to end the collaboration?
COMMUNICATION between partners	• What level of respect and trust exists between the partners? • Is communication open and frank, and is critical communication constructive? • How is communication between the partners managed? • Does each partner have a partner relationship manager? • What channels and vehicles are used to communicate internally? • Are there potential dissenters, and can they be converted? • How does the alliance communicate externally? • Do the partners have a coordinated external communication strategy and program? • Is the partnership underpublicized?
CONTINUAL learning	• What has each partner learned from the collaboration about how to work with another organization more effectively and create greater partner and social value?

Exhibit 8.1. The Seven C's: Questions for Partners, Cont'd.

	• How has this learning been incorporated into the collaboration? • Is there a process for routinely assessing learning from the collaboration? • Is complacency stifling innovation?
COMMITMENT to the partnership	• What is the level of organizational commitment to the partnership and how is this commitment demonstrated? • What is the trend in investments (personal, financial, institutional) in the partnership? • Are the partners' expectations of one another high? • Are partner expectations and commitments commensurate with execution capabilities? • What is the composition of each partner's collaboration portfolio, and where does this alliance fit within those portfolios? • Are the portfolios consistent with the partners' collaboration capacities?

Note: Prepared with the assistance of Linda Carrigan.

Notes

Chapter One

1. Quotations from company and nonprofit personnel for which no published source is cited are taken from interviews conducted by the author and his research team.

2. H. Schultz and D. J. Yang, *Pour Your Heart into It* (New York: Hyperion, 1997), p. 300.

3. Boston baseball fans are still waiting hopefully for the Red Sox to be world champions.

4. H. J. Ferguson, "New Realities for Nonprofits," *Business and Economic Review*, July-Sept. 1994, 4(4), 29–30.

5. J. B. Sterns, "Joint Venture Is Practical Approach to Use of High-Tech Equipment," *Trustee*, Aug. 1992, 45(8), 16–18.

6. L. A. Harvey, "Public-Private-Nonprofit Partnerships for Breaking Welfare Dependency," *National Civic Review*, Winter 1993, 16–24.

7. American Association of Fund-Raising Counsel Trust for Philanthropy, *Giving USA* (New York: American Association of Fund-Raising Counsel, 1998).

8. C. Smith, "The New Corporate Philanthropy," *Harvard Business Review*, May-June 1994, 105–116. Intensifying global competition and the growing complexity of business are also leading companies to turn increasingly to business alliances; R. M. Kanter, "Six Strategic Challenges," *World Link*, Jan.-Feb. 1998, 28–34, has identified alliances among corporations as a key trend and imperative in the twenty-first century.

9. J. E. Austin, "The Invisible Side of Business Leadership," *Leader to Leader*, Spring 1998, 8, 36–46; "Corporate Community Service:

Achieving Effective Engagement," Harvard Business School Working Paper, 98–21 (Boston: Harvard Business School, 1997).

10. S. A. Waddock and S. B. Graves, "The Corporate Social Performance: Financial Performance Link," *Strategic Management Journal,* 1997, *18*(4), 303–319; D. Lewin and J. Sabater, "Corporate Philanthropy and Business Performance," in D. F. Burlingame and D. R. Young (eds.), *Corporate Philanthropy at the Crossroads* (Bloomington: Indiana University Press, 1996).

11. Conference Board, *Corporate Volunteer Programs: Benefits to Business,* Report No. 1029 (New York: Conference Board, 1993).

12. R. Steckel and R. Simons, *Doing Best by Doing Good: How to Use Public Purpose Partnerships to Boost Profits and Benefit Your Community* (New York: Dutton, 1992), p. 25.

13. For further elaboration of the benefits of community engagement see Austin, "The Invisible Side of Business Leadership," 36–46, and R. M. Kanter, "From Spare Change to Real Change," *Harvard Business Review,* Apr.-May 1999, 122–133.

14. For an insightful analysis of partnering among businesses, see R. M. Kanter, "Collaborative Advantage: The Art of Alliances," *Harvard Business Review,* July-Aug. 1994, pp. 96–108; Kanter also richly delineates fifteen skills needed to achieve "collaborative advantage," in R. M. Kanter, *World Class: Thriving Locally in the Global Economy* (New York: Simon & Schuster, 1995).

15. For a more academic treatment of the material, with fuller references to related theoretical literature, see J. E. Austin, "Strategic Collaboration Between Nonprofits and Business," *Nonprofit and Voluntary Sector Quarterly, 29* (supplemental 2000).

Chapter Two

1. A. R. Andreasen, "Profits for Nonprofits: Find a Corporate Partner," *Harvard Business Review,* Nov.-Dec. 1996, 47–59; Cone Communications and Roper Starch Worldwide, *Cause-Related Marketing Trends Report* (Boston: Cone Communications and Roper Starch Worldwide, 1997).

2. Although Timberland stock is publicly traded, corporate control remains in the Swartz family, with Jeff Swartz representing the third generation managing the company.

3. H. Schultz and D. J. Yang, *Pour Your Heart into It* (New York: Hyperion, 1997), p. 296.

4. Schultz and Yang, *Pour Your Heart into It,* p. 296.

Chapter Three

1. Data for Community Wealth Ventures are drawn from the author's research for a Harvard Business School case: M. D. Pearson and J. E. Austin, "Community Wealth Ventures, Inc.," 9-399-023, Aug. 5, 1998.

2. H. Schultz and D. J. Yang, *Pour Your Heart into It* (New York: Hyperion, 1997), p. 295.

3. Schultz and Yang, *Pour Your Heart into It,* p. 295.

Chapter Four

1. H. Schultz and D. J. Yang, *Pour Your Heart into It* (New York: Hyperion, 1997), pp. 296, 300.

Chapter Five

1. A. R. Andreasen, "Profits for Nonprofits: Find a Corporate Partner," *Harvard Business Review,* Nov.-Dec. 1996, 47–59, points to several risks for nonprofits that partner with corporations, including damaged image, undue influence on the nonprofits' programs, displacement of traditional donors, and financial overdependence.

2. "Broken Deal Costs A.M.A. $9.9 Million," *New York Times,* Aug. 2, 1998, p. 12 col. 6; C. E. Bartling, *Strategic Alliances for Nonprofit Organizations* (Washington, D.C.: American Society of Association Executives, 1998), pp. 49–53.

3. R. Abelson, "Marketing Tied to Charities Draws Scrutiny from States," *New York Times,* May 3, 1999, p. 1.

4. S. Gray and H. Hall, "Cashing In on Charity's Good Name," *Chronicle of Philanthropy,* July 30, 1998, p. 25.

5. Gray and Hall, "Cashing In on Charity's Good Name," p. 25.

6. M. Burros, "Endorsements Raise Money and Questions," *New York Times,* Oct. 22, 1997, p. 3.

7. Cone Communications and Roper Starch Worldwide, *Cause-Related Marketing Trends Report* (Boston: Cone Communications and Roper Starch Worldwide, 1997).

8. See, for example, D. F. Burlingame and J. M. Hodge (eds.), *Developing Major Gifts*, New Directions for Philanthropic Fundraising, no. 16 (San Francisco, Jossey-Bass, 1997); A. Kihlstedt and R. Pierpoint (eds.), *Capital Campaigns: Realizing Their Power and Potential*, New Directions for Philanthropic Fundraising, no. 21 (San Francisco, Jossey-Bass, 1998); D. A. Brehmer (ed.), *Communicating Effectively with Major Donors*, New Directions for Philanthropic Fundraising, no. 10 (San Francisco, Jossey-Bass, 1995); J. E. Nichols, *Transforming Fundraising: A Practical Guide to Evaluating and Strengthening Fundraising to Grow with Change* (San Francisco: Jossey-Bass, 1999); M. Carlson, *Winning Grants Step by Step: Support Center of America's Complete Workbook for Planning, Developing, and Writing Successful Proposals* (San Francisco: Jossey-Bass, 1995); S. L. Golden, *Secrets of Successful Grantsmanship: A Guerrilla Guide to Raising Money* (San Francisco: Jossey-Bass, 1997).

9. For additional rich examples of corporations using their core competencies to create social value and accrue strategic business benefits, see R. M. Kanter, *Business Leadership in the Social Sector*, H13S Enterprise Video Series: IBM Reinventing Education, no. 399-502; Bell Atlantic in Union City, no. 399-501 (Boston: Harvard Business School Publishing, 1998).

10. One of the companies new to the alliance had previously donated twelve miles of its river frontage to the DNR.

11. R. M. Kanter, *When Giants Learn to Dance* (New York: Simon & Schuster, 1989), p. 160, cites such an imbalance in a business-to-business partnership as a potential "dealbuster."

Chapter Six

1. C. W. Letts, W. P. Ryan, and A. Grossman, *High Performance Nonprofit Organizations: Managing Upstream for Greater Impact* (New York: Wiley, 1998).

The Author

James E. Austin is the John G. McLean Professor of Business Administration at the Harvard University Graduate School of Business Administration, where he has been a member of the faculty since 1972. He is chair of the Harvard Business School Initiative on Social Enterprise and teaches and researches social entrepreneurship, strategic management of nonprofits, and nonprofit board governance. Austin, whose work as a scholar and teacher has been acclaimed in such publications as the *Financial Times*, the *Wall Street Journal*, and the *New Yorker* magazine, is the author of fifteen books, dozens of articles, and a multitude of case studies. For the past three and a half decades, he has served as an adviser to businesses, nonprofit organizations, and governments throughout the world.

Index

Leader to Leader

A quarterly publication of the Drucker Foundation and Jossey-Bass Publishers

Frances Hesselbein, Editor-in-Chief

Leader to Leader is a unique management publication, a quarterly report on management, leadership, and strategy written by today's top leaders *themselves*. Four times a year, *Leader to Leader* keeps you ahead of the curve by bringing you the latest offerings from a peerless selection of world-class executives, best-selling management authors, leading consultants, and respected social thinkers, making *Leader to Leader* unlike any other magazine or professional publication today.

Think of it as a short, intensive seminar with today's top thinkers and doers—people like Peter F. Drucker, Rosabeth Moss Kanter, Max De Pree, Charles Handy, Esther Dyson, Stephen Covey, Meg Wheatley, Peter Senge, and others.

Subscriptions to **Leader to Leader** are $149.00.
501(c)(3) nonprofit organizations can subscribe for $99.00 (must supply tax-exempt ID number when subscribing). Prices subject to change without notice.

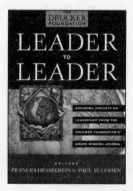

Leader to Leader

Enduring Insights on Leadership from the Drucker Foundation's Award-Winning Journal
Frances Hesselbein, Paul M. Cohen, Editors

The world's thought leaders come together in *Leader to Leader*, an inspiring examination of mission, leadership, values, innovation, building collaborations, shaping effective institutions, and creating community. Management pioneer Peter F. Drucker; Southwest Airlines CEO Herb Kelleher; best-selling authors Warren Bennis, Stephen R. Covey, and Charles Handy; Pulitzer Prize winner Doris Kearns Goodwin; Harvard professors Rosabeth Moss Kanter and Regina Herzlinger; and learning organization expert Peter Senge are among those who share their knowledge and experience in this essential resource. Their essays will spark ideas, open doors, and inspire all those who face the challenge of leading in an ever-changing environment.

For a reader's guide, see www.leaderbooks.org

Hardcover 402 pages   ISBN 0-7879-4726-1   Item #G379 $27.00

FAX	**CALL**	**MAIL**	**WEB**
Toll Free 24 hours a day: 800-605-2665	Toll Free 6am to 5pm PST: 888-378-2537	Jossey-Bass Publishers 350 Sansome St. San Francisco, CA 94104	Secure ordering, tables of contents, editors' notes, sample articles at www.josseybass.com or www.leaderbooks.org

Lessons in Leadership

Peter F. Drucker

Over the span of his sixty-year career, Peter F. Drucker has worked with many exemplary leaders in the non-profit sector, government, and business. In the course of his work, he has observed these leaders closely and learned from them the attributes of effective leader-ship. In this video, Drucker presents inspirational por-traits of five outstanding leaders, showing how each brought different strengths to the task, and shares the lessons we can learn from their approaches to leadership. Drucker's insights (plus the accompanying *Facilitator's Guide* and *Workbook*) will help participants identify which methods work best for them and how to recognize their own particular strengths in leadership.

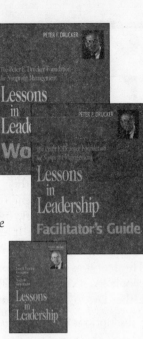

1 20-minute video + 1 *Facilitator's Guide* + 1 *Workbook*
ISBN 0-7879-4497-1 $89.95

Excellence in Nonprofit Leadership

Peter F. Drucker, Max De Pree, Frances Hesselbein

This video package is a powerful three-in-one development program for building more effective nonprofit organizations and boards. *Excellence in Nonprofit Leadership* presents three modules that can be used independently or sequentially to help nonprofit boards and staff strengthen leadership throughout the organization. The video contains three twenty-minute programs: (I) *Lessons in Leadership* with Peter Drucker (as described above); (II) *Identifying the Needs of Followers*, with Max De Pree and Michele Hunt; and (III) *Leading Through Mission*, with Frances Hesselbein. The video comes with one *Facilitator's Guide*, which contains complete instructions for leading all three programs, and one free *Workbook*, which is designed to help participants deepen and enrich the learn-ing experience.

1 60-minute video + 1 *Facilitator's Guide* + 1 *Workbook*
ISBN 0-7879-4496-3 $129.95

FAX
Toll Free
24 hours a day:
800-605-2665

CALL
Toll Free
6am to 5pm
PST:
800-956-7739

MAIL
Jossey-Bass Publishers
350 Sansome St.
San Francisco, CA
94104

WEB
Secure ordering at:
www.josseybass.com

The Drucker Foundation Self-Assessment Tool

Since its original publication in 1993, the best-selling *Drucker Foundation Self-Assessment Tool* has helped and inspired countless nonprofit boards, executives, and teams to rediscover the direction and potential of their organizations. This completely revised edition of the *Self-Assessment Tool* now offers even more powerful guidance to help organizations uncover the truth about their performance, focus their direction, and take control of their future.

The *Self-Assessment Tool* combines long-range planning and strategic marketing with a passion for dispersed leadership. It allows an organization to plan for results, to learn from its customers, and to release the energy of its people to further its mission. The *Process Guide* by Gary J. Stern provides step-by-step guidelines and self-assessment resources, while the *Participant Workbook* by Peter F. Drucker features thoughtful introductions and clear worksheets. Participants will not only gain new insights about their organization's potential, but also forge strategies for implementation and future success.

Multiple Uses for the *Self-Assessment Tool*

- *The leadership team*—the chairman of the board and the chief executive—can lead the organization in conducting a comprehensive self-assessment, refining mission, goals, and results, and developing a working plan of action.

- *Teams throughout the organization* can use the *Tool* to invigorate projects, tailoring the process to focus on specific areas as needed.

- *Governing boards* can use the *Tool* in orientation for new members, as means to deepen thinking during retreats, and to develop clarity on mission and goals.

- *Working groups from collaborating organizations* can use the *Tool* to define common purpose and to develop clear goals, programs, and plans.

Process Guide   Paperback ISBN 0-7879-4436-X $29.95
Participant Workbook   Paperback ISBN 0-7879-4437-8 $12.95

1+1 SAT Package = 1 *Process Guide* + 1 *Participant Workbook*
ISBN 0-7879-4730-X $34.50 **Save 20%!**

1+10 SAT Package = 1 *Process Guide* + 10 *Participant Workbooks*
ISBN 0-7879-4731-8 $89.95 **Save 40%!**

FAX
Toll Free
24 hours a day:
800-605-2665

CALL
Toll Free
6am to 5pm
PST:
800-956-7739

MAIL
Jossey-Bass Publishers
350 Sansome St.
San Francisco, CA
94104

WEB
Secure ordering at:
www.josseybass.com

Leading Beyond the Walls

Frances Hesselbein, Marshall Goldsmith,
Iain Somerville, Editors

from the Drucker Foundation's Wisdom to Action Series

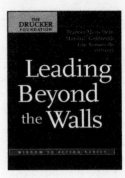

"There is need for acceptance on the part of leaders in every single institution, and in every single sector, that they, as leaders, have two responsibilities. They are responsible and accountable for the performance of their institution, and that has to be concentrated, focused, limited. They are responsible however, also, for the community as a whole. This requires commitment. It requires willingness to accept that other institutions have different values, respect for these values, and willingness to learn what these values are. It requires hard work. But above all, it requires commitment; conviction; dedication to the Common Good. Yes, each institution is autonomous and has to do its own work the way each instrument in an orchestra plays its own part. But there is also the 'score,' the community. And only if the individual instrument contributes to the score is there music. Otherwise there is only noise. This book is about the score."

—Peter F. Drucker

Increasingly, leaders and their organizations work in ways that extend beyond the walls of the enterprise. These partnerships, alliances, and networks allow organizations to achieve new levels of performance. At the same time, they create new challenges. Leaders "beyond the walls" must be adept at building and maintaining relationships, comfortable in working with individuals and organizations they cannot control, and able to move beyond the old preconceptions.

Leading Beyond the Walls presents insights from over twenty-five thought leaders from all three sectors, exploring the challenges and opportunities of partnership as well as the unique practices and perspectives that have helped individuals and organizations become more effective.

Hardcover   ISBN 0-7879-4593-5 $27.00

FAX	CALL	MAIL	WEB
Toll Free	Toll Free	Jossey-Bass Publishers	Secure ordering at:
24 hours a day:	6am to 5pm	350 Sansome St.	www.josseybass.com
800-605-2665	PST:	San Francisco, CA	
	800-956-7739	94104	